How to Get Into Medical School

By Someone that has Actually Done It

By

Daniel W. Mijares, M.D.

ISBN 978-1-4303-2680-9

ISBN 978-1-4303-2680-9

Dedication

To Alba, Michelle, Isabella and the rest of my family.

Thank you for all of your understanding, trust and support.

Also, a special thanks to all of the pre-medical students

that have encouraged me to do this book.

Table of Contents

HOW TO GET INTO MEDICAL SCHOOL

Getting into medical school is very difficult and has many twists and turns, especially if you plan on entering directly following graduation from college. I have put together some steps to help you succeed in this matter. What follows are some useful steps to improve your chances of getting in.

What you're getting into

So you're thinking about becoming a doctor? Their will always be a need for doctors because people will always get sick. However, this field draws to it a certain kind of person. My first piece of advice to you is this, don't make this decision lightly. You are talking about a lifetime commitment. If you are doing it for money, fame, or prestige, you should think again. With the state of medicine today, doctors do not make as much money as they have in the past, and most people only see physicians as people to help them and serve their needs when they want. Once you have decided to go to medical school, it will impact the rest of your life. This includes all of college, medical school, residency and working after that.

You should think through your decision carefully. Talk about it with your family and friends and any people whose opinions you respect. Speak to your science professors and any physicians you know. Your professors have had you in class and can give you a good idea of how they think you would handle the stress of medical school. Take some time to reflect. Ask yourself if this is really what you want to do, and try to follow your heart and instincts. The decision to pursue a career in medicine should be made only after careful thought, assessment of your personal motivation and realistic assessment of the demands of medical training and practice. People who enjoy their careers in medicine enjoy helping sick people and are willing to take responsibility for the lives of others. These people are committed to a life of service and never ending education.

Many factors can affect your decision to apply to medical school and make it more difficult. Some people may want to take a break after finishing school. Others may need to work to pay off debts or loans. Or maybe you just don't know what you want to do with your life for sure. Think hard about why you want to go into medicine. Is it the financial security, the desire to help others, the intellectual curiosity, research, wanting to find a cure for a disease, or one of other several reasons that interests you? Make sure this is well thought out because admissions committees look at that intensely. Your motivation for becoming a doctor will shape the way you go about achieving your goals. If you do it for genuine reasons, people will likely recognize it. The same applies if you are doing it for the wrong reasons. Keep in mind, there are many easier ways to make money than to go through medical school, residency and never ending continuing medical education. M.B.A.'s take only two years of your life, cost much less than four years of med school, and you will get paid much better for several years after you get out. Whatever your reasons for going to med school just make sure they are from the heart.

For these people, it is especially important to discuss their thoughts, ideas and hopes with other people. The Academic Advising Center of your school or college is a great starting point. These advisors can help you make decisions about a career path, education path and even coursework needed to get where you want to be. You should also visit the websites of the professional organization for all allopathic medical schools in the United States: The Association of American Medical Colleges, the professional organization for all osteopathic medical schools in the United States: The Association of American Colleges of Osteopathic Medicine, and write to medical schools for their catalogs to give you an idea of the curriculum and training they provide. Other people's brains you can pick include professors, physicians, and current medical students. There is no substitute for obtaining first hand information about the field and what you may be in for.

The second piece of sage insight is: don't let anyone stop you from going after your dream. You don't have to ignore what people are telling you, just think about the things they say and why they are saying. Most people you are talking to do not want you to fail, so if someone is telling you something that seems difficult to swallow, take a look and see if that's true. However, don't let anyone say to you that it's too difficult and you will never succeed, for whatever reason. I firmly believe that we can do anything we set our minds to. So if this is truly what you want to do, you believe you can do it, and you're mature enough to handle the challenge, then do it.

Now that you've decided to go for med school, you should know that the application process is very long, complicated, and expensive.

Medical school and the training that follows will take seven to eleven or more years of school beyond your bachelor's degree. You will also be investing considerable financial resources (about $30,000 a year or more in most cases) in your education and training, not including life expenses such as food and shelter.

In the end, it is important to make a well-thought out decision. Don't go to medical school expecting the excitement you see on televisions shows and don't go if you're not sure that you want to go. If you have carefully thought out your options and choose to go to medical school, you will find a stimulating and challenging career that can provide a lifetime of rewards.

It is a great time to enter the medical profession. There are continuous technical advances. Furthermore, it is a time of serious attention to the needs of society including preventative care, promotion of wellness, and the continuing debate of medical ethics. With all the struggles to get good grades, have the best MCAT scores, having great experiences and obtaining letters of recommendation, the mission of the medical profession is often lost, but should not be.

Medicine was developed out of a need to care for people in the most basic and the most complex ways possible. Despite its place in the eyes of many in society today, medicine is one of the noblest professions. It allows people to help others live better. It allows for the exploration of illness and health. It is easy to lose track of these goals when you are performing the incredible number of tasks needed to accomplish this goal. As you progress through the process, keep your goals in mind and let the nobility of the profession provide meaning for you.

The application process to medical school is physically and emotionally demanding. It is also time-consuming. The process has become more difficult by the fact that medical schools are becoming increasingly competitive. Only about 35% of the people who apply to medical school are admitted. Also, the number of applicants to medical school also continues to increase. To become a successful medical school applicant, you will need to be organized, plan ahead and utilize all the available resources.

While preparation for medical school will obviously take significant amounts of your time and energy, don't forget to make the most of your undergraduate education and have fun. No one wants to miss out on the greatest years of their lives.

Medical School Admissions: The Process

Getting in into a medical school is difficult. But for the most part, you can control your fate.

The truth is, you're set if you can get a high GPA, an extremely high MCAT, write a fantastic personal statement and do well on the medical school admissions interview. Your admission to medical school is virtually guaranteed if you also have good recommendations, have done community service, and have an uncle who is the chair of an admissions committee.

However, despite everyone's best efforts, it is essentially impossible to do all of these things. The good news for you is that no one on the admissions committee really expects you to do all of that. Doing some of the things well is good enough.

The secret to doing this is knowing what you can control and then doing it. Your inspiration should always stay high.

For most of us, being successful depends on setting the right goals and priorities and tirelessly following the path to success. Just remember, life dose not always cooperate with us, and despite your best intentions, your GPA or MCAT score may be less than you wish it were. Take heart, life is not over yet.

Lessons in Strategy: Getting into medical school

Lesson 1: Most schools and their computers will first look at your numbers (the objective data): your GPA and MCAT scores. Each school views these differently and weighs the importance individually. Some think GPA is more important, others give more value to the MCAT. However, if both, or oftentimes, even one of these does not meet the schools minimum requirements, which vary from school to school, your application will likely not even be seen by a human being or the light of day. If this is the case, it does not matter how many awards you have won or how good your extra-curriculars are. If you GPA and MCAT do not meet the standards, no one will know of your other accomplishments. As such, you need to maximize your GPA and MCAT.

Moral of Lesson 1: GPA and MCAT are the highest priority items. They rule and all else falls in line.

Lesson 2: The MCAT is a tough exam, no doubt about it. The secret to success is doing well in pre-med classes, assuming your school's classes are rigorous. This is better than cramming and trying to learn the information later. It will serve to increase your GPA and studying for the MCAT. A significant portion of the questions on the MCAT, approximately 75-90%, depending on the rigor of your school, could be answered with the knowledge of the required premed courses. If you buckle down and make some sacrifices and do well in those premed classes, you will reap the benefits of having a high Science GPA. This will also put you on the road to a good MCAT score. If you performed less well, you can still study on your own and prove to the schools that you can do the work by doing well on the MCAT. Of course, in an ideal world, you will do well in your courses and on the MCAT.

Again, note that about 75-90% of the MCAT questions are covered in typical pre-med courses. That leaves 10-25% of the questions on the MCAT that will not be covered in typical courses. This is what separates a good score from a great score. This will affect not only if you can get into medical school, but where you can get in.

If you're a science major, you may cover some or all of the remaining percentages in your other science classes, but you might not. The best bet is to get the MCAT Manual which lists all the topics covered on MCAT well before you plan to take MCAT. In fact, you should get it when you are a freshman or sophomore at the latest. You should make note all the topics that you did not cover in your classes and study them on your own or with a tutor. You can even then arrange your schedule to take classes where you will learn this stuff if needed. This early planning will give you great advantage later, not only in studying and preparation, but in decreasing your stress level.

You should not only take your pre-med biology classes because these will only cover a small portion of the biology content tested on MCAT. You should also take Human Physiology, if available. Genetics is definitely a class that should be taken. Again, check out the MCAT Manual and be sure to cover the topics you don't know. This is where the organization comes in. You will require advance planning since you will not be able to cover everything the night or even the month before MCAT.

You should also work hard in your classes because when you apply to medical schools using the general AMCAS application, most schools will send you their own "secondary" application. Most schools secondary applications ask to list pre-med courses with grades. The schools do this to simplify their lives. All medical schools receive thousands of applications for a limited class size. Admissions people need a way to quickly eliminate people and use this as another screen to get through.

If you did poorly in one class, don't worry. Getting admitted to medical school is not just science, but a confluence of forces. Some people who have done poorly in a class or two get in, and others that have not done poorly in any classes, do not get in. Life is not fair, plan appropriately.

Moral of Lesson 2: The best preparation for MCAT is doing well in your pre-med classes. This requires lots of planning and follow through of the process.

Are you qualified?

Admission to medical school is very competitive. On an average, each medical school will get anywhere from 5,000 to 14,000 applications for classes ranging from 45 to 295.

The numbers are stacked against you and you need to have some basic qualifications to even be *considered* for an interview.

The average scores and GPAs have steadily increased from year to year, and I do not believe that trend should change anytime soon. Getting into medical school is tough and it takes work. You should keep a few things in mind as we begin this journey.

Are your GPA and MCAT scores adequate?

The average applicant to medical school has GPA and MCAT scores of 3.5 and 27 respectively. The average student accepted to medical school has GPA and MCAT scores of 3.7 and 30 respectively. If your numbers are significantly below these, chances are you will not even get an interview, much less get into medical school. If you are below average, save your time and money and improve your credentials before applying.

As you can see, the standards are very high: Less than half of all applicants get accepted in any given year. This should not be a source of discouragement, but one of motivation. It tells you what you're up against. Now is the time to make your plans to succeed on the MCAT and in your remaining classes. Also remember, the interview counts for a lot as well.

For the purposes of medical school admissions there are actually TWO GPAs that you need to keep in mind: The science GPA and the non-science GPA. These are calculated as follows:

1. Science GPA: This is calculated by taking into account all classes you took in Math, Biology, Chemistry, Physics, etc. You do not choose what classes you want to count for Science GPA, but remember you can choose the classes you take. This is more important than your Non-Science GPA, but your Non-Science GPA is important as well.
2. Non-Science GPA: Calculated by taking into account all other classes that are not used in calculating your Science GPA.

Pre-med Requirements

Admission to medical school requires taking the MCAT and specific course.
Many high quality extra-curricular activities may not be required, but are needed to be a competitive applicant. Several schools will not only consider you a poor applicant if do not list many extracurriculars on your application, they will also not interview you.

What medical school admissions committees look for

Approximately 70% to 80% of the admissions decision depends on your GPA and MCAT scores alone. However, there is more to the admissions decision. The emphasis placed on the different parts of your overall application will vary from school to school. Some medical schools emphasize the MCAT and don't consider much else, while other schools take the MCAT as only part of the application and it will only eliminate someone whose scores are very low. Some schools place all their emphasis on extra-curricular activities and a well-rounded application.

The following (the order of which varies depending on the school) are the main areas used by admissions committees to evaluate candidates:

1. GPA
2. MCAT scores
3. Application material
4. Recommendation Letters
5. Personal Interview

The letters of recommendations are usually written by people such as faculty, physicians or managers who have interacted with you in extra-curricular activities or in the classroom. Therefore, these really reflect how you did in the activities that you listed on your application.

Some medical schools won't consider you if you have never been in a clinical setting, because they want to know: How would you know what physicians do, or that you like what physicians do?

A few schools require that you do some research - without it, they will not consider your application, either. Other schools may not care about research at all. So, a lot depends on the specific medical schools you are interested in.

It is best to prepare as if you needed to cover all of the areas mentioned well. This will make your application strong, regardless of which schools you end up sending your application.

The role GPA plays in Medical School Admissions.

A GPA is often used to screen out candidates. Some use certain GPA cut-offs others use the ever guarded formulas that incorporate GPA and MCAT scores to initially screen out applicants before letting actual people to look at individual applications. If your GPA is not up to snuff, you might not even get looked at, despite all of your other accomplishments. In fact, many schools will not even send you their secondary applications if you do not pass the first screening test.

Medical schools look closely at your science GPA and the grades you received in the required science classes. The admission committees know that the premed requirements are tough and they often use these courses to gauge your ability to handle medical school.

It may be unfair, but it's the truth. There are many people who are extremely smart and who would make great physicians, but for some reason could not get the "numbers" right to get into medical school.

You can always try to explain your circumstances, and hopefully medical schools will listen. This is more likely acceptable if you had one semester that was poor, but performed well all the other times. In some circumstances, you may want to consider some backup plan or alternative options, which may include getting a graduate degree and doing really well so that you can show that you can indeed do well academically in the proper setting. Another option is to apply to DO Medical Schools, which allows you to become a Doctor of Osteopathy (DO) instead of Doctor of Medicine (MD). You can apply to MD and DO schools at the same time, but they require different applications, even though both require the MCAT. Doing extremely well on MCAT may improve your chances of getting in, but your GPA is highly important and a high MCAT score may or may not cut it alone.

DO schools seem to be more flexible on evaluating applicants, which is an advantage if you have had a few slip ups. The disadvantage is that you get a DO, which is, in all rights, similar to MD. However, there are very few DO's and no one really knows much about them. It also carries some stigma with it in the medical community. Many people consider it slightly less than an M.D.

Do you have significant volunteer and research experiences?

Most medical schools expect applicants to have significant volunteer and/or research work.

Most medical schools put a strong emphasis on exposure to medicine related work, such as internships or research experiences. Get started as soon as possible. It's never too early to start looking for internships. Some people even start at the end of high school. This is your competition, so get started early. Research experience is helpful as well. Try to do a summer research program or job. Which ever one of these things you do, make sure it has meaning to you and it is something that you enjoy.

Community service is probably the most important, easiest, and most rewarding thing you can do. While doing community service in and of itself will not get you into medical school, it will help your application and will give back to you in many ways.

Often, what distinguishes a good applicant from an excellent applicant is the strength of their extracurricular activities. Medical schools look not only for involvement, but also for leadership. It is better to get involved and have leadership roles in a few activities that interest you rather than to be involved in a thousand things without doing much for any of the organizations you belonged to.

Employment while in school can also be a plus. Working your way through school and paying for your own education shows responsibility and maturity. These are characteristics that medical schools love.

Even though high grades are important, getting into the medical school of your choice doesn't require endless days and nights spent studying, locked away from civilization. In fact, doing so may put you at a disadvantage when interview day rolls around. Medical schools do like to see a strong GPA and a high MCAT score, but these are simply criteria they use to eliminate the pool of applicants down from several thousand to a few hundred. Good scores are important because they will get you in the door and get you to the interview. But once you get an interview, you will need your social and communication skills to show that you can make it. You aren't going to find those skills by spending four years locked away studying. After all, medicine is a social, interactive profession.

You make yourself an attractive, well rounded candidate simply by doing things that you enjoy. Do things that you are passionate about and it will come across in your application and interview.

When looking through your list of extracurricular activities, medical schools want to see a picture of someone who enjoys what they do, not just someone who joins clubs and does work to put them on their Curriculum Vitae. It doesn't pay to spend time on activities you hate just because you think they are going to get you into school. Your lack of enthusiasm will show during the interview, and you will have wasted possibly the best years of your life doing something you didn't like, which may actually be worse.

It is helpful if you have done activities that have benefited others. Helping others is what medicine is all about, and it can make for great stories. It could be tutoring school children, helping the elderly, working on a political issue that is important to you, or advocating some cause.

In the end, what really matters is your personal accomplishment. What you have achieved and what you have learned. Remember, failures also count because they teach you important lessons. Don't be afraid to talk about your failures, but always talk about them in a positive note, not dwelling on how you failed and how bad you felt. Talk about how the situation made you learn and how you would do things differently in the future.

All of this should be fantastic news. Enjoy your time in college, make the best grades you can, and you'll be happy. Creating a list of extracurricular activities is like a job, you should do things you enjoy. Then, getting up everyday is like going to work at a job you love. You'll need to talk about yourself a lot during the interview process, and having experiences that make you a memorable interviewee are very important.

Experience

Successful candidates to medical school usually are people who have demonstrated that they know how to function in a clinical environment. Having some sort of clinical experience on your application is essential. Medical schools look for this to ensure that you really know what you are getting in to. This requirement isn't hard to meet. Shadowing a physician, doing medical research in the summer, volunteering or working at the office of a physician, in the department of a hospital or at any other kinds of facilities that care for people, such as an assisted living facility, nursing home or a battered women's shelter and volunteering your time at a clinic for the underprivileged are all ways to gain experience in the medical field. Obtaining these experiences in the office of a primary care physician is excellent because these practices see a wide variety of patients ranging from healthy people to seriously ill people who require considerable care. Most people applying to medical school don't know much about the medical field, but having had some experience of the lifestyle before applying would be an advantage to the admissions committee.

It is very useful to the medical school applicant to obtain a letter of recommendation from this volunteer experience, if it was a good one. Thus, it is good to have one physician get to know you well enough so that he or she feels comfortable writing a letter on your behalf. Many students do their volunteer work in the office of a physician they already know, such as their former pediatrician or the physician of a family member.

For those that want to volunteer in a hospital setting, you should call the volunteer services office of a local hospital. Do not be afraid to express interest in working in a particular department, such as the emergency department or cardiology, but don't be discouraged if you do not receive your first choice.

Even though you are volunteering, it is important that you act professionally and responsibly in every aspect of your assigned duties. The relationships that you develop will become an important part of your medical school application as recommendations from volunteer supervisors will reflect your job performance.

You can use your time as a volunteer to assess whether being a physician is what you want to do. Talk to the people with whom you work and find out what they like and do not like about what they do. This is the time to think about whether this is the lifestyle you are interested in pursuing or not.

Volunteer for as long as you can. This will show medical schools that you are serious about the profession. It is best to start this as soon as possible. You may want to vary your work by trying different volunteer work experiences and settings. You can try working in the hospital, in a private office or do research. These types of experiences will show medical schools that you have knowledge of several areas and are open to new experiences.

Volunteering should not take a large amount of time away from your studying or MCAT preparation. Even a small amount if time each week over several months can give you considerable clinical experience and can help a supervisor get to know you enough a to write an excellent medical school reference letter.

What do admission committees expect you to gain from clinical experiences?

They want you to understand what it takes to care for others. They want the applicant to see the realities of working with sick people so that you know what you're getting yourself into for the rest of your life. They also want to know what you have learned about yourself and other people by working with the sick.

If you can tell a story about how a particular experience influenced you and what you have learned from it, that is ideal. Don't try to make things up. People can usually see through that easily.

Helping other human beings is the heart of what medicine is about. Some of what will set you apart as an applicant are those things that show traits such as compassion and caring. Volunteering to help others will add positively to your perspective on life, not just add to your CV. One of the things people look for in a doctor is a sense that he cares about them as people. This is a skill that cannot be taught, but volunteering to help others will certainly help.

Shadowing

This is one of the best extra-curricular activities because it provides you with clinical exposure and stories to talk about in the interview. It also allows you to see what medicine and a physician's life are like. Most people have an idyllic view of this, but you can see the reality. The good, the bad, and the ugly. You will also get a good sense if medicine is really for you.

If you are still thinking about the answer to "Why do you want to go into medicine?", I would suggest doing more shadowing. Spend a fair amount of time getting to know the physician, the specialty and medicine. Be sure to spend enough hours shadowing the same physician to get to know him and the field better. Again, don't forget to enjoy this opportunity to be in a clinical setting while working through the pre-med coursework.

How Do You Set Up Shadowing

You can set up your shadowing however you like. Some people like to shadow a few hours every week for several weeks or months. Some people spend time with one physician for an entire week in one stretch to get a better idea of what it's really like.

To schedule your shadowing, pick the specialty you are interested in shadowing and call any physician's office. This can be someone you know or even someone you don't know. Tell the office person that you are a pre-med student at your university and are planning to go to medical school and would like to shadow the physician if possible.

Ask them if the doctor allows students to come into the office to shadow him or her. Usually, they have done this before with other students and the physician has no problems with this. Tell them what dates you are available to shadow. Usually, the office help will take down your phone number and then call you back later, after asking the physician or office manager.

To follow a surgeon into the operating room, you may have to obtain permission from the hospital or surgery facility as well as the patient. You can tell the physician's office staff that you'd like to follow the surgeon in the office, in the OR and on rounds if possible. They usually know if there are obstacles for you. Some hospitals and facilities have special rules and regulations and may require you to sign some paperwork.

The physician you are shadowing is the key to get you into the OR and on the hospital floors. The physician will typically let everyone know that you are with him or her. Most of the time, that's enough justification for you to be there.

When Shadowing

This may seem obvious, but make sure you are dressed and groomed professionally when shadowing. If there is any question, overdress until you can get a feel for what is acceptable in the office or the physician tells you it is okay to dress down. For men, that should be dress pants, shirt and tie. For women, dresses or professional business attire should be okay.

Most of the time, you just stand back and observe what the physician does without doing much yourself. It is important to stay out of the way. After all, that's what shadowing is. Some physicians may involve you to some degree, but don't expect too much.

It is important to actively ask questions between patients or when appropriate. It is not appropriate to ask questions during the exam if not prompted. You want plenty of interaction with the physician so the physician can get to know you and sees you are interested in medicine. At the end, ask the physician for a great letter of recommendation. You should do this right away while you are still fresh in the physicians mind. Don't underestimate the importance of the letter and asking for it, because there is a right and a wrong way to ask for a letter.

Volunteer and Service

You may wonder why this is important. Physicians are, after all, in the business of helping people.

So, you say you want to help people? This will likely be a question during your interview. Can you show that you mean it, or is this just talk?

Volunteering and participating in service opportunities are a few ways to demonstrate your commitment to help others. Volunteer tutoring, summer camps, soup kitchens, hospital or clinical volunteer work, shoveling snow off driveways, church service, missions, etc, all work to show that you care about helping people during your pre-med preparation. Ideally, you participate in more than one type of activity.

Do whatever is interesting to you or get involved in a cause that you can personally gain satisfaction from. You may be asked in your interview why you got involved in what you chose.

Many people have already begun giving back to the community and are involved in specific projects involving the poor, elderly, underprivileged, sick, or children and adolescents who are in great need and in danger of slipping through the cracks in society. If you are already involved, then continue with what you are doing.

If you are extremely short on time, or even if you are not, you may want to try to find activities that will help you participate in volunteer or service opportunities while at the same time gaining valuable exposure to a clinical setting. For example, try to volunteer in a clinic or hospital. Your hours spent are considered clinical exposure time and volunteer time when it comes to your application. Especially if your time is limited, this is a great way to go.

Medical missions and other service or relief projects are also a great way to get involved in very intense service. For most students these are life-changing opportunities, being exposed to extreme poverty, different cultures and customs. You may or may not be able to participate in providing medical care, but rather be involved in the project in various ways. Medical missions and various other relief projects are often organized by student or professional groups at universities. There are also different religious and non-religious groups that organize service missions and medical missions. Most often, you have to pay your own way (this can be a few hundred to a few thousand dollars), but frequently these organizations also provide some assistance to help you find a sponsor for your trip. Overall, these can be very fulfilling and humbling experiences.

However you do it, volunteer, paid or by shadowing, make sure that you do enough of it. Talking about your experiences drawn from clinical exposure are guaranteed interview topics. They also provided you with reasons and excitement for choosing medicine. You will have specific situations, patients, etc. to talk about (without disclosing private information) in your interviews.

These experiences and their impact on you, the things that "make you tick," are the things that interviewers are interested in because it gives them a view into your thoughts and feelings about medicine.

Research

There is one other thing that is pretty much non-negotiable on resumes these days: research. Many medical schools pride themselves on it, and they want to see that you've tried your hand at it as well. Tried is the key word here. Some medical schools don't care at all whether you have done research or not. However, most medical schools prefer to see some research experience on your application and yet other schools absolutely require it and won't consider you if you have done little or no research. Generally speaking, some minimal exposure such as working in a research lab for a semester is okay for most schools.

Yes, they will be impressed if you come to them touting a possible cure for cancer, but they will also be impressed if you can talk intelligently about some investigation of athlete's foot or arthritis that you did over a summer, with or without significant scientific findings. Once again, find something that you are really interested in researching. These experiences, while not earth-shattering in the eyes of the scientific community, provided plenty of perspective on medicine, and plenty to talk about in essays and interviews. Some schools may expect you to have published something. You must demonstrate to the committee that you have accomplished something meaningful.

The toughest part of doing research, other than perhaps the writing of your final paper, is figuring out what to do, and how to sign up for it. If you live in a city with a medical school nearby, there will usually be a summer research program of some type that allows undergrads to participate. If there are no medical schools nearby, there are certainly doctors, and there are probably some doctors who wouldn't mind having someone shadowing them at work from time to time. Ask that doctor if there is any way to do a small research project with him or her, and they will probably be able to at least point you in the right direction. And as for undergraduate research during the school year, a few telephone calls will probably put you in touch with the right person to speak with about that, and you may even find that you get some academic credit for your research.

However, as already mentioned, some schools want to see major research involvement, perhaps that you have done your very own project, and may prefer published work. Especially if applying to research top medical schools, this will probably be necessary.

Some professors help undergraduate students set up their very own research projects that lead to publication of their work in the end. Others involve students in ongoing projects or use them as grunt workers to care for animals or have them clean their labs. All intermediates between these two extremes are possible.

To strengthen your application for most medical schools, the goal here is to:

1. Be involved in thesis driven research

2. To be able to explain what the "goals" of the project were

3. Show what you did to contribute and what your responsibilities were

4. Be able to give some background and detail in your interview

Again, schools that are big into research will probably put more focus on research than other medical schools. Make sure you prepare appropriately. Find out if the medical schools you are interested in have specific requirements or a reputation for requiring research or expecting research of students - and how much of it.

Leadership and Multitasking

Leadership

This is an area that includes things like tutoring, student government positions, supervisory positions (can be at work or elsewhere) of any kind, church or other teaching assignments and positions, military service or anything like it. It's beneficial to be able to show these on your application.

Most medical schools consider these good experiences that will strengthen your application.

Multitasking

Medical school is hard work. You are enrolled in courses totaling about 24 credits per semester of upper division science courses with labs. If you have only taken 12 credits per semester during undergrad, you need to be able to show that you have kept an otherwise busy schedule, indicating that you could handle 24 credits per semester if you had to. If 12 credits per semester took all of your time and maxed you out, medical school will probably be a bit much.

Showing that you worked 20-40 hours a week, took 12 credits and did various other activities for some number of hours each week shows that you can handle it and that you can multitask. Balancing family responsibilities (if you have kids) also counts as time spent multitasking and is justification for having taken a less intense class load during undergrad.

So, bottom line, you don't have to take 24 credits during undergrad in any one semester, but be sure to demonstrate that you can handle a busy schedule in your life.

Characteristics Sought in Applicants

- **Positive sense of self or confidence**
  Integrity
  Strength of character
  Determination
  Independence

- **Realistic self-evaluation and introspective capabilities**
  Recognize shortcomings
  Works hard to improve
  Responsibility for your own shortcomings or is there always an excuse?
  (Do you own up?)

- **Prefers long term goals and is not into immediate gratification**

- **Consistency in academic and personal life**
  Course loads taken
  Solid performance or an upward trajectory
  Multi-tasking

- **Staying Power**
  What is your pattern of involvement with extra-curricular activities?
  When things get tough what is your reaction?

Coping techniques

Stamina

- **Leadership Experience**

  What is your style of leadership?

- **Community Service**

  When, where, how long?

- **Demonstrated Medical Interests**

  Work, internships, volunteer opportunities in medical settings

  When, where, how long?

  What is your motivation toward medicine and how strong is your motivation?

- **Team Player**

  Shares

  Plays well with others

  Competitive

  Responsibility to a group

- **Communication and Interpersonal Skills**

  How do you handle difficult social interactions?

  Can you keep confidences?

  How do you discuss grade discrepancies?

  How do you handle team research projects?

  Are you willing to:

  Seek help

  Accept help

  Ask questions of instructors

  Try different approaches to study

- **Adaptability**

  How do you handle new environments?

  How do you handle different teaching styles?

  Have you lived in another country? How did you handle it?

- **Cultural and Social Sensitivity**
  How do you interact with people from different ethnic, cultural, and socioeconomic backgrounds?

Have you completed the necessary pre-medical coursework?

Almost every medical school requires the following courses, and though not explicitly stated, expect you to have obtained high marks in each of them: Introduction to Biology (two semesters), General Chemistry (two semesters), Organic Chemistry (two semesters), and Physics (two semesters). A significant number of schools also require 4-6 courses in the humanities (e.g., English, History, Philosophy, etc.), and many require a year of calculus. You should always determine a school's requirements before you apply.

Note that some medical schools require courses such as Biochemistry or additional Calculus, for example. Other special non-science courses may also be required by some medical schools.

Higher-level biology or other science courses are often encouraged but not required. There is no preference for a science major over others, as long as you have completed the required courses. So take on a major that interests you in college: this is the time to do that.

It is important to note that you do not have to be a science major to apply to medical schools. In fact, sometimes medical schools prefer candidates who are academically well-rounded. However, scientific thinking and reasoning skills are important, especially for purposes of taking the MCAT, and good grades in science courses will show medical school admissions committees that you are likely to be able to handle the basic intellectual challenges of medical training.

If you get a poor grade in one of your science courses, you have not destroyed all chances of getting into a medical school. One single poor grade will not prevent an otherwise strong student from gaining admission to medical school. Most medical schools are understanding of and even sympathetic to aberrations in students performance, particularly if the struggle occurred early during their college career.

Almost all medical schools require you to have a four year degree before applying. However, some schools offer premed programs which provide students the opportunity to prepare for medical school without gaining a four year degree. This program often takes three years to complete.

Nowadays, medical schools look for individuals from diverse educational backgrounds. Therefore, you should take a breadth of courses from social science and humanities to natural science. Remember that undergraduate may be your last chance to touch on social science and humanities courses.

Although the choice of your major doesn't affect your acceptance at all, you must complete the following basic natural science courses in order to show your ability to handle heavy science course-load in medical school.

This table is based on statistics from AAMC:

Required Subjects	Number of schools (over 110 schools) requiring these subjects
Physics with lab	107
Inorganic Chemistry with lab	105
Organic Chemistry with lab	104
English (College composition)	74
Biology or Zoology	55
General Biology	53
College Calculus (1 year)	22

College mathematics	21
Behavioral and/or social sciences	16
Humanities	15

Consult particular medical schools (or look at their web sites) to find out the specifics.

Pre-med requirements play a very important role in admissions for several reasons.

1. Pre-med requirements make the bulk of the science classes you will take in college and determine your Science GPA, which is one of the determinants of your chances of admission.
2. You will need to get recommendations for medical schools from science faculty, and if you do not take other science classes, getting them from professors who taught pre-med classes will be your only option.
3. Pre-med requirements cover most of the material you need to know for the MCAT. The better you know the stuff covered in these premed classes the better off you're when the time comes for taking MCAT.
4. Schools ask you explicitly to list premed requirements along with your grades on their secondary applications, which means they bear a lot of weight.

Having completed a Master's Degree or PhD is advantageous for admissions and may give you an edge by making you stand out from your peers, but is not required by any medical school for admission. These degrees are especially helpful when applying to some of the more prestigious medical schools.

Where to find specific medical school requirements

You should order the medical school admissions guide for both allopathic (MD) and osteopathic (DO) schools for the most current requirements of each school. You can also check medical school websites directly.

The Osteopathic Medical School Information Book (DO) is available for free. You can browse through the guide online or order a free copy to be sent to you.

The Medical School Admission Requirements (MSAR) for MD schools is available for a small fee.

Note that these guides will not elaborate on the extra-curricular "requirements" as discussed here, but list cost of tuition, course requirements and the like. The MD school guide also included numerous statistics such as how many people applied in-state and out-of-state, how many of those were interviewed and were admitted, etc. These publications are very useful tools.

Acing Premed Requirements

There is an obvious way to succeed in your premed classes: work hard. This is obvious and true for all classes.

Yet science classes that make up the premed requirements are different from all others. For one, they are the lifeline to your medical career. They also require a different approach than let's say History, Psychology or Anthropology.

In all your science premed classes: Chemistry, Organic Chemistry, Physics, Calculus and to some extent in Biology, the difference between a good grade and a bad grade is not necessarily knowing stuff. You can read Chemistry all you want and know every tiny fact about it, but the chance is that this alone will not ensure you a good grade.

The "secret" to doing well in these classes is:

- Understanding the topics, theory, etc
- doing practice problems

Without doing MANY practice problems you will NEVER do well on the exams. Most exams I've seen are structured to test problem-solving ability and this is also true of the MCAT. So, do spend the extra time practicing solving actual problems. Get a solution manual for your textbook and check yourself.

For Organic Chemistry and Physics, you should be aware that often there is more than one correct way to solve a problem. The solution manual for your textbooks will usually give only one approach. You would know if you solved it correctly in Physics because if you did you will get the same numbers. In organic chemistry, there is no way for you to know for sure if your "alternative" solution is correct because even though you may have gotten the right result, your methods may be erroneous. I would recommend that you take your solution to your professors or TAs and ask them to look at it. You will derive two benefits from doing so: (1) you will know if you solved problems correctly, and more important, (2) if you did not solve it correctly, you will understand why your approach is erroneous and does not work.

The secret for getting a high GPA

Are there secrets for getting good grades? If you ask your parents they will probably tell you to go back to your room and study harder. They are right. But I think this is not the end of the story.

Studying day after day can eat you up fast. The biggest secret I know to keeping yourself sane while spending significant portion of your life in the library is exercise. Really, spend an hour or half an hour a day or every other day in the gym, go jogging, go to the pool. Keep yourself physically fit. Working out actually affects and improves your thinking--it gets your blood flowing and brings the much needed oxygen to you brain. It also gives a boost of energy that is especially needed during the exams. You cannot realize how valuable and important exercise is until you have done it for some time.

I know it sounds ridiculous, but instead of cramming 12 hours a day for five days during the finals, spend one hour each day at the gym. I bet you will immediately feel the difference. You will not lose that hour because you will in fact be studying more productively the other 11 hours. One of the common characteristics of very successful high-level business executives (who usually work 70-80 hours a week) is that they exercise regularly.

Time management is crucial

You need to choose a setting where you study best. I found from experience that oftentimes the worst way to study is in a group or in proximity to people. You end up talking a lot, answering questions from people who have not done the work and working on areas that are not your weakness. It is a waste of time. Out of two hours of study you may only get 15 minutes of productive information going to your brain. I'm not advocating that you become a sociopath. In fact, I think having social life is essential to good performance. What I'm saying is that it may be well worth it to separate your academics from your social life. You will be much better off if you spend two hours intensely studying and then spend two hours socializing than if you spend four hours mixing socializing with studying. At the end of four hours of social-studying you will have neither learned much nor socialized too well.

Set priorities. Always keep your short-term and long-term goals in sight.

To accomplish your goals, you must accept the trade-offs. We can't all be business majors.

You must always keep your long term and short-term goals in sight. You must also realize that oftentimes your goals are not the same as the goals of your friends. This means that you cannot always do what your friends are doing. To accomplish your goals you must accept the trade-offs. In addition, it is important to note that different goals require different trade-offs. Again, I'm not advocating that you become a sociopath. What I am saying is that if your goal is to get into medical school and your friend's goal is to be a big-shot Wall Street broker, you must realize that you may have to study when he or she goes partying. Why? For one, because if you always do what he or she does, you may end up being a big-shot Wall Street broker instead of being a doctor. Different goals require different trade-offs.

How can I get a high GPA? How can I raise my GPA?

First, as I previously mentioned, the grades you get in premed classes are very important. For that reason, you might want to take them one or two at a time and do really well on them. It is a lot of work and your GPA is much more important than getting over these classes.

Some people are also known to have taken the difficult premed classes at schools other than where they get their BA/BS and where the standards are lower--just be careful with that because this might raise a flag on your application. In the best case you will be asked why you took a class at a different school during the interview and hopefully you will give a satisfactory explanation.

Another alternative is to take the hard premed classes during the summer. Beware though that summer classes are very intense and they cover material very fast--so there is no opportunity to relax. If you don't do the work for a few days in classes such as Organic chemistry, Biology or Physics during the summer session, you might get a poor grade whereas you can get away with it during the regular semester.

If you have already taken your premed requirements and did really poorly in one or two classes, which can totally ruin your GPA, I suggest that you find out the policies of your school regarding retaking classes. If your school totally removes all traces of your previous grade from your transcript, as I know some schools do, then by all means retake the class.

On the other hand some schools will not remove the previous grade from the transcript if you retake the class. They just added the new grade along with the old grade. In this case, you may still want to retake that one science class you did poorly in just to prove to the admissions that you know your stuff. On the other hand, you may just try to maximize your GPA. In particular, if your science GPA is low, you might want to consider taking some of the science classes that are commonly taken by the athletes at your school--no prejudice--but athletes tend to have a sixth sense for easy classes. In other words, take the low-level easy classes from science departments (Biology, chemistry, physics, math). Usually these do not satisfy requirements for science majors but you will not have to do much work for these classes and you will still be able to list them as "science" classes for the purposes of your science GPA calculations when applying to medical schools.

Now I do not recommend that you waste your college career taking this kind of classes. It is much better to take higher level classes and do well in them. But when you're in a desperate situation and need to pull up your GPA--this is a good way to go.

The following is the summary of very basic techniques for grade point success. Although these techniques are really simple, people often fail to practice them, and the students without good study habits are often those who complain about the difficulty of the course.

- **Obtain old exams**: You can get old exams from upper classmates, teaching assistants, or even the professors. Remember that the professors sometimes are not creative enough to change the formats or even the contents of their exams every term. Therefore, studying these exams beforehand provides you some ideas on what will be on the new exams.
- **Take a reasonable course load**: Reasonable schedule means more time to concentrate on your classes. You will have a chance to enjoy your classes and study them in depth.
- **Study alone**: In most circumstances, studying alone is the best way to get higher grades because it helps you avoid unnecessary discussions on some irrelevant topics with your study partners.
- **Choose a proper study environment**: Library-like environment is where you could study efficiently because it is quiet, and most people seem to study very hard there.
- **Highlight your books**: This is the good way to filter out minor details, and it's also an excellent way to preview for exams.
- **Make flash cards**: This technique is most useful, but less used, technique. It triggers your long term memory deeply. Anyone who's been through biology class could see the power of this technique in learning biological terms.
- **Keep a social life**: Social relaxation provides an excellent release for tension and prevents burnout.
- **Understand concepts that seem unlikely to appear on the exam**: These concepts are what your professor writes extra credit questions on. So, if you want to be a stand-out of the class, make sure you touch on these questions.
- **Don't memorize when you can understand**: Generally, it's less efficient to memorize many details than to understand a general principle from which you can derive the specifics.

The school you attend is also important. A college with a tough academic reputation is likely to impress an admissions committee. The most important thing in college is to learn as much as you can, in and out of the classroom because you will probably not have an opportunity quite like it at any other time of your life.

Study hard and play hard. If you need academic help ask for it. Many colleges have extensive academic advising programs. Use the resources available to you. At the same time try not to stress out too much about school work and have fun. There were too many people in my college that obsessed enormously about grades and forgot the importance of just learning and having fun. If you are struggling and feel burnt out you may want to lighten your academic load (no one says you need to graduate in four years. Maybe you can do a semester or a year overseas. Special programs during college (like semesters away and co-op programs) can impress admissions officials and also provide a source for letters of recommendation. Get to know your professors and get involved in class. Professors will be writing letters for you and you want to impress them with your stellar class participation and outstanding academic skills. Don't get discouraged if you started out slowly in college. Improving your GPA from year to year also counts for a lot. A less than stellar first two years in college can be made up to some extent with a good finish. Post-baccalaureate programs allow people who have their bachelor's degree to take pre-med requirements. A good show in these courses can also show med schools that you can handle the work. Remember to do your best and learn the most you can.

Questions to Assess Your Study Habits

While not everyone can accomplish all of these ideas for good study, they are highly effective, and the more you acquire, the more you will take from your courses.

Do you study in a location and area that is conducive to concentration, minimal interruptions, and focused study?

Do you review your notes from a specific class that same day (taking advantage of your short term memory) to fill in the gaps and clearly identify your questions? Do you leave room in your notes to enter additional information?

Are you able to carve out a minimum of 4 hours a day, 6 days a week, to study?

When you have an hour between classes, do you take advantage of the time (e.g. to review notes)? Have you inventoried and evaluated how you use your time in a typical day?

Do you know which hours during the day you are best able to concentrate for intense study and which hours are least conducive? How much time do you waste in a day?

Do you keep a regular daily schedule? Do you try to avoid getting up early some days and sleeping late others?

How far in advance of a test do you begin the process of reviewing/studying? Do you have a system for condensing material, remembering material, and testing yourself?

Do you have an efficient means of keeping track of what needs to be done and what your priorities should be weekly? Daily? Do you keep short and long term goals?

Do you attempt to set up and/or participate in study groups when appropriate?

Do you see your teachers during their regular office hours? Have you ever shared your approach to studying with your professor (particularly if you are having problems)?

How much do you study extraneous material that ends up not being covered in class or on a future test?

Do you find time each day to do something for you (exercising, reading, etc)?

Undergraduate Time Line

Freshman Year

- Explore various fields of study.
- Do well in classes.
- Think about career interests.
- Volunteer during school breaks in a health related organization.
- Read science journals
- If you've already decided to try medicine as a career, start taking science classes now--like chemistry.

Freshman year is a time to explore your new school. Don't be too concerned with your post-graduate training yet; there's still a lot of time. However, it is important to do well academically from the start, so you should make academic success a high priority. Also, it is never too early to explore volunteering at a hospital or physician's office as a way of learning about different fields of interest to you.

In addition, if you feel it is necessary, you may want to take non-credit courses in improving study skills, reading capacity, and time management. Students should also begin reading scientific publications and other professional journals. Not only does exposure to the information and writing styles found in these publications improve your knowledge about current topics in science, but the technical writing style will prepare you for the type of reading you will need to become proficient in for your science courses and throughout medical school. In addition, the writing style and subject areas will be similar to passages you will encounter during the MCAT.

Your freshman year is also an excellent time to get involved in an extracurricular activities. By doing this, you will have the opportunity to feel more a part of the community, reap many rewards and make a contribution to your community and yourself. There are organizations which are academically based, leisure based, community service based, and activist based.

The most important policy during your first year is not to over-commit yourself. It cannot be stressed enough that your priority is your classes and schoolwork. Do not allow yourself to be spread so thin among your activities and responsibilities that you do not have the needed time to devote to your classes.

Sophomore Year

- Choose a major.
- Continue completing the required science courses.
- Talk to health professionals about their careers.
- Volunteer part-time or during school breaks in a health related capacity.
- Begin arranging an independent study with a professor for your junior year.
- Make an appointment to meet with a pre-med advisor to discuss various health professions and plan your course of study.
- Do well in classes.
- Get to know professors and get letters of recommendation.

By your sophomore year, you should be narrowing down some fields of interest. You should choose a major this year. Make it an area about which you enjoy learning. Medical schools do not require undergraduate degrees in science, and there is little difference in acceptance rates for science versus non-science majors. It should be noted, though, that students who take courses in the sciences beyond the minimal prerequisite courses for medical school generally have a higher rate of acceptance than those students who take only the required introductory chemistry, organic chemistry, physics, and general biology with no other science courses. In whatever field you decide to pursue, you should seek a curriculum that will afford you academic rigor and sharpen your skills in reading, writing, analytical thinking, research, and public speaking. Course load and performance throughout are significant to the admissions boards no matter your major.

Talk to faculty and professionals in different fields to help you evaluate possible careers. If you did not begin as a freshman, start taking the requisite science classes and make an appointment during spring semester to plan your course of study with an academic advisor. Start making contacts with professors and ask for letters of recommendation if you have made a good impression. Keep your GPA high. This is an important piece of your application which can be forgotten.

Junior Year

- Meet with a pre-health advisor to discuss your academic record and extracurricular activities.
- Register to take the MCAT in the Spring or Fall.
- Study for the MCAT or take a prep course.
- Do well in classes.
- Continue to volunteer.
- Check websites or write to medical schools for catalogs and decide where to apply.
- Download and begin working on the common medical school application from http://www.amcas.org.
- Schedule a pre-med interview with a Pre-Health Academic Advisor
- Prepare financial information for submission to schools for determination of financial aid.

This the most exciting year for students that want to start medical school in the Fall following graduation. It is also the busiest and most stressful. So prepare yourself. If you haven't already, you should make an appointment to speak with an academic advisor about your courses, identifying the medical schools to which you will apply, your extracurricular activities, and your letters of recommendation. Now is the time to start getting your whole application package in order.

You will probably take the MCAT in the Spring, so you need to plan ahead and budget your time to prepare. Keep current with your coursework (do not get behind). Apply early for the MCAT, and begin studying for them at least four to six months in advance. If you desire, take a prep-course for the MCAT, but no matter how you prepare, be ready. It is not advisable in most cases to re-take the MCAT.

As a junior, you should also be finalizing your decisions about where to apply and finishing your applications. Scheduling a pre-med interview with a Health Professions Advisor is highly recommended both as a way for you to practice your interviewing skills and as a way to get a comprehensive letter of recommendation from the Advising office sent to medical schools along with your other application materials.

The time following your spring semester of your Junior year you should begin working on your personal statement. Once you have carefully created it, and feel it is strong, you should have it checked by someone who's writing style you respect for comments and suggestions.

Of course, doing well in your courses and gaining work experience continue to be priorities during your junior year.

Senior Year

- Finish applications.
- Interview at individual schools if invited.
- Make a back-up plan.
- Keep G.P.A. up.

If you are invited to interviews, spend time preparing for them. Most interviews occur between September and March of your senior year. Final decisions may not be made until the spring or even summer for students placed on waiting lists.

In the beginning of the year, you should double check that you will meet your graduation requirements.

After you have completed the interviews, the application process is complete. Don't forget to consider your alternatives, though, in case your medical school plans don't work out this year.

Specific School requirements

Some schools are more specific than others in specifying what activities are required or are just good to have to make your application stand out from the pack. The list of requirements or recommendations should look about the same for most medical schools. Some research powerhouses may have larger research requirements than your average schools. There may even be various lists available from different schools, but most don't spell out their requirements very well.

In order to qualify for an interview, a candidate has to meet at least the average values in most of the categories. This is a summary of information obtained from many schools. The Average reflects the true average for all of their applicants each year. Performing below the minimum in any one category automatically disqualifies applicants from receiving interview invitations.

Category	Minimum	Average
GPA	3.0	3.7
MCAT	21	30
Shadowing	1 day	3 days
Volunteer/Service	3 hrs/week for 3 months	4 hrs/week for 4 years (no typo)
Clinical Exposure	4 hrs/week for 2 months	4 hrs/week for 3 months
Research	4 hrs/week for 2 months	4 hrs/week for 3 months
Leadership Positions	1 in past 3 yrs	3 for 3 months each in past 4 yrs
Multitasking		20 hours per week

Time spent in these areas can overlap. For example, volunteer tutoring hours would be considered leadership and volunteer time. Time spent in a volunteer clinic would count as volunteer/service time and clinical exposure.

The weaker your MCAT score and GPA, the more important are all the other areas to strengthen your overall application. If your MCAT or GPA are average or below average, you will need to make your application stand out in other areas. This allows you to prove to the admissions committee that you have something to offer that is not reflected by your MCAT score and GPA alone.

The goal of all of this

Your goal is to score well on the criteria the admission committee uses to evaluate you and gain admission to the school. Having spent plenty of time in each of these areas makes you a much stronger applicant and shows the school that you are serious about medicine.

Again: Why should you do all of these?
To make you a better applicant.
To make you stand out from the pack of applicants.
To show them you are serious about medicine.

So, your MCAT and GPA are average? (If you don't know your score yet, prepare as if it was average - and you cannot go wrong with your preparation)
Is there anything else you can show the admissions office that they should choose you over someone with a higher GPA and MCAT score than you?
Yes: all kinds of hours spent in extra-curricular activities to demonstrate your commitment.

Your activities demonstrate your commitment to the admissions committee. All these extra activities look good on your application and may make it stand out from the rest.

Perhaps you could also argue that most everyone does those things, so you really can't stand out. All the more reason to do them so you are not behind your competitors. Not all applicants do these, so you do have a chance to stand out.

You can pick one area that you really like and spend way more time there to stand out. If you love research, try to invest years there instead of months. If you love shadowing, put in hundreds of hours instead of 20 hours only. If you can't stand out everywhere pick one area to do it. I personally think you can beat the averages listed in the table previously in all categories fairly easily.

The importance of your undergraduate college or university.

Generally speaking, the better your undergraduate school, the better for you and your pursuit of getting into medical school. So, graduating from a top school with your Bachelor's degree will make things easier for you than graduating from some community college or less well known school. This still holds true even if you get a lower GPA at the top school than you would at the community college.

Admission committees look at the school you attended and consider this when they analyze your GPA. So, someone who graduated from Harvard may only have a 3.2 GPA and someone at a community college may have a 3.9 GPA. They may have about equal chances for admission to a certain medical school when looking at their GPA alone since most schools factor in the difference in school difficulty and quality of education obtained. Obviously, this is also just comparing the extremes here. Most schools fall in between these extremes.

Realize that you will see some people in medical school who have only attended community colleges or state schools rather than top undergraduate schools. Like everything that is part of your application, the school you attend can help you. Also note that your school may be more important if you are trying to go to medical school at one of the top schools in the country.

According to some pre-med advisors, your undergraduate institution is of extreme importance, but generally speaking, I think this is somewhat overrated, unless you are trying to get into one of the most prestigious medical schools, as already mentioned.

The best advice is to try to get into the best undergraduate school you can. It will only help you. But realize that it's not going to be the end of the world if you attend a less well known school. The rest of your application may have to be a little stronger in that case, but you should still be able to get into medical school.

Try to choose an undergraduate institution which has successfully graduated students who were able to gain admission to medical school. Ideally, your school should have a pre-med advisor and committee as well as a strong Pre-med or Biology program. Of course, attending a smaller community college will be a disadvantage because they typically don't have strong programs of this type.

This is more important than how well known the school is. Try to stay away from schools which have no track record or a bad track record of getting pre-med students admitted to medical school. It will make things harder for you, but still not impossible.

The premed department

At this point, you may already have chosen your undergraduate major and decided to stick with it for good. However, if you're still undecided, I'd like to say a few words about the benefits offered by a strong premedical program, if one is available at your particular university. A good undergraduate premed department will do a number of things for you, and they may vary slightly from school to school, but they usually include the following:

1. A detailed outline of what should be done in each semester to prepare yourself for application to medical school.

2. Periodic meetings to discuss your class's progress and preparation for application. This may include one-on-one meetings with an advisor.

3. A central office, through which all of your application materials (letters of evaluate, transcripts, etc.) will flow.

4. Guidance in the application and interview process, including helpful hints and perhaps even recommendations about particular schools suited to you.

5. A number of research opportunities, both through the school and with alumni who often offer nice stipends and interesting projects.

6. Notification of scholarship opportunities for premedical students.

If medical school is your goal, and you're sure of it, I would recommend a premed major instead of a major in one of the sciences, like biology. The guidance offered by a department whose sole purpose is to assist you in getting into medical school should not be underestimated. If something else interests you, there's always the option of double-majoring.

If you don't want to, or can't, major in some kind of pre-medical program, a comparison of performances on the MCAT for applicants and matriculants, grouped by undergraduate major, is available on the AAMC website.

Advice for non-premeds

Alright, so you've decided that you can't take the type-A's in the premed department and you've set out for a journey through biochemistry or art history instead. You can still get into medical school without being premed, or so you've been told. Really, you can, but you'll need to be aware of a few things that your premed department would have otherwise taken care of for you.

1. Pay attention to your timetable. You won't have someone telling you which courses to take and when to take them, so make sure that you get the core material that will be on the MCAT out of the way before you take the test. That core material would be: basic courses in biology, organic chemistry, physics, general chemistry, and, if possible, a basic course in genetics.

2. If your school doesn't have a premed committee, it more than likely doesn't have a preprofessional major. Make sure that you are able to cover your major's courses with the courses you need to take the MCAT in order to avoid the stress of taking a ridiculous course load at the last second in order to finish out all of your requirements and graduate.

3. Based on the last point, you won't have someone there to make sure that you've met all of the necessary pre-requisites for coursework for applying to medical school. While most schools require the same major areas, some differ in duration and type of courses. For example, a biochemistry course is sometimes required. Make sure to check the websites of the schools you are interested in to see which courses you will need to take prior to matriculating.

4. You won't have a committee to write a letter for you. This is not a big deal, but just keep that in mind when you are totaling up your letters of evaluation. If you feel you need a letter of this type, see if your school has a health sciences counselor or similar position who has dealt with this situation before.

5. More on the letters of evaluation: You may need to have these sent in to the medical schools individually by the professors, since you won't have someone there to gather them and send them in a group. Just make sure that the people writing your letters are following the correct form and guidelines as pertains to each individual school.

6. If you need advice on which schools to apply to, or whether or not to retake the

MCAT, check out your career services center. If they can't help, they more than likely know who can, and can direct you to that individual.

Post Bachelor Pre-Med Programs

Post-Bac Pre-Med programs can be useful for two types of individuals in particular:

1. An individual who completed his or her Bachelor's degree, took the MCAT, applied to medical school and did not get in.

These programs can help improve an applicants chances for admission for several reasons:

  a. They improve the student's science background, increasing chances for better MCAT performance.

  b. They show that the student is serious about getting into medical school.

  c. They prepare the student for medical school and are typically more intense than undergrad - showing that the applicant can handle a more rigorous course load just fine. Some of these already teach a number of courses found in medical school itself for that reason - demonstrating that the applicant can handle it.

2. An individual who has already completed a Bachelor's degree in a non-science field (or it's been a long time since graduating) and would like to prepare for medical school now.

This option should be weighed against just returning to a regular university to take the required courses needed for medical school admissions and MCAT preparation. Technically, it's not necessary to go to a post-bac pre-med program per se.

You could just as well enroll at any university for 2 years to take 2 semesters of Physics, 2 semesters of General Biology and 2 semesters of General Chemistry followed by 2 semesters of Organic Chemistry.

On the other hand, some students are successfully admitted to medical school after completing one of these programs when whey were previously unable to gain admission several times through the normal route. So, these programs seem to be able to make a difference for some applicants.

Medical Schools with Math Requirements

- University of Alabama: 6 semester hours of college mathematics; calculus is recommended
- Univ. of South Alabama: 8 semester hours of college math required; calculus is "Highly recommended"
- Univ. of Arkansas: 2 semesters mathematics; calculus is recommended
- Univ. of California, Davis School of Medicine: 2 semesters of college math is required
- Univ. of California, Irvine College of Medicine: 1 semester of calculus is required
- Univ. of California, Los Angeles UCLA: 2 semester of math is required; calculus is recommended
- Univ. of California, San Diego: 8 semester hours of math is required; calculus is recommended
- Keck School of Medicine: Some college math and calculus is recommended
- Stanford Univ.: Some calculus is recommended
- Univ. of Colorado: 6 semester hours of college math is required
- Univ. of Connecticut: Some college math and calculus is recommended
- Georgetown Univ.: 3 semesters of college math is required
- Howard Univ.: 6 semester hours of college math is required
- Florida State Univ.: 6 semester hours of college math is required
- Univ. of South Florida: 2 semesters of college math is required
- Morehouse School of Medicine: 2 semesters of college mathematics is required
- Southern Illinois Univ.: 2 semesters of college mathematics is required

- University of Chicago: Some calculus is recommended
- Univ. of Iowa: 1 semester of college math is required
- Univ. of Kansas: 1 semester of college math is required
- Univ. of Louisville: 2 semesters of college math is required
- Louisiana State Univ, New Orleans: 6 semester hours of college math is recommended; calculus is recommended
- Johns Hopkins Univ.: 6 semester hours of calculus is required
- Uniformed Services Univ.: 3 semester hours of calculus is required
- Boston Univ.: 2 semesters of calculus is recommended
- Harvard Medical School: 2 semesters of calculus is required
- Univ. of Massachusetts: Some calculus is recommended
- Michigan State Univ.: 3-4 semester hours of college math are required
- Univ. of Minnesota-Minneapolis: 1 semester of calculus is required
- Univ. of Mississippi: 6 semester hours of college math is required ; 3 semester hours of calculus is recommende
- Univ. of Missouri – Colombia: 3 semester hours of college math is required
- Washington Univ.: 2 semesters of calculus is required
- Univ. of Nebraska: 3 semester hours of calculus is required
- Univ. of Nevada: Some college math and calculus is recommended
- Dartmouth Medical School: 3 semester hours of calculus is required
- UMDNJ – New Jersey Medical School: 1 semester of college math is required
- UMDNJ – Robert Wood Johnson Medical School: 1 semester of college math is required
- Albert Einstein College of Medicine: 6 semester hours of college math is required
- Mount Sinai: 2 semesters of college math is required
- SUNY Upstate Medical Univ.: Some calculus is recommended
- Univ. of Rochester: 1 semester of college math and calculus are recommende
- Duke Univ.: 2 semesters of college math is required
- Univ. of North Dakota: 3 semester hours of college math is required
- Medical Univ. of Ohio: 2 semesters of college math is required
- Northeastern Ohio Univ.: Some college math and calculus is recommended

- Univ. of Cincinnati: Some college math and calculus is recommended
- Wright State Univ.: 2 semesters of college math is required
- Oregon Health Sciences Univ. School of Medicine: 1 quarter of college math is required
- Jefferson Medical College: Some college math is recommende
- Pennsylvania State Univ.: 2 semesters of college math is required
- U of Penn: Some college math and calculus is recommended
- Univ. of Pittsburgh: a strong background in mathematics is highly recommended
- Universidad Central del Caribe: 6 semester hours of college math is required; calculus is recommended
- Ponce School of Medicine: 6 semester hours of college math is required
- Brown Univ.: 1 semester calculus is required
- Univ. of South Dakota: 2 semesters of college math is required; calculus is recommended
- Texas A & M Univ. Health Science Center: 3 semester hours of calculus is required
- Texas Tech. Univ.: 3 semester hours of calculus is required
- Univ. of Texas Southwestern Medical Center at Dallas: 1 semester of calculus is required
- Univ. of Texas Medical School at Galveston: 1 semester of calculus is required
- Univ. of Texas – Houston Medical School: 6 semester hours of college math is required
- Univ. of Texas Medical School of San Antonio: 3 semester hours of calculus is required
- Univ. of Utah: Some college math and calculus is recommended
- Univ. of Vermont: Some college math is recommended
- Virginia Commonwealth Univ.: 2 semesters of college math is required
- Medical College of Wisconsin: 4 semester hours of college math is required
- Univ. of Wisconsin: 2 semesters of college math is required

Medical Schools Recommending a Statistics Course:

- Loma Linda University
- University of Massachusetts
- University of Minnesota
- University of Rochester
- Oregon Health & Science University
- University of Pennsylvania
- Brown Medical School
- Texas A&M University (required)
- Texas Tech University (required)

Medical Schools Requiring Advanced Science Courses:

- Univ. of Alabama: Biochemistry and genetics are recommended
- Univ. of South Alabama: Biochemistry is recommended
- Univ. of Arkansas: Biochemistry and genetics are recommended
- Keck School of Medicine, Univ. of Southern California: Biochemistry and molecular biology are required
- Loma Linda Univ.: Biochemistry is recommended
- Stanford Univ.: Biochemistry is recommended
- Univ. of California, Davis: Biochemistry and genetics are recommended
- Univ. of California, Irvine: Biochem and another upper division class are required. Genetics is recommended
- Univ. of California, San Diego: Biochemistry and genetics are recommended
- Univ. of Colorado: Biochemistry and genetics are recommended
- Univ. of Connecticut: Biochemistry, genetics, and physiology are recommended
- Georgetown Univ.: Biochemistry is recommended
- Florida State Univ.: 6 semester hours of biochemistry is required. Genetics is recommended
- Univ. of Florida: Biochemistry is required

- Univ. of Miami: 6 semester hours of other science is required. Biochemistry is recommended.
- Emory Univ.: Biochemistry is recommended
- Medical College of Georgia: 1 semester of advanced chemistry is required. Biochemistry is recommended.
- Mercer Univ.: 2 semesters of biochemistry are recommended
- Morehouse School of Medicine: 1 semester with lab of biochemistry and genetics are each recommended
- Univ. of Hawaii: Cell biology with lab and biochemistry are required. Genetics is recommended
- Loyola Univ. Chicago: Genetics is recommended
- Southern Illinois Univ.: Cell/molecular biology and physiology & microbiology w/lab are required. Biochemistry is recommended.
- Univ. of Chicago: Biochemistry w/lab is recommended
- Univ. of Illinois at Chicago: Genetics is recommended
- Univ. of Iowa: 1 advanced course in biology is required
- Univ. of Kansas: Biochemistry and genetics are recommended
- Univ. of Louisville: Genetics is recommended
- Louisiana State Univ. New Orleans: Biochemistry and genetics are recommended
- Louisiana State Univ. Shreveport: Biochemistry and genetics are recommended
- Boston Univ.: Biochemistry, genetics, and molecular biology are recommended
- University of Massachusetts: Biochemistry is recommended
- Michigan State Univ.: 1 upper level biology course is required. Biochemistry and genetics are recommended.
- Univ. of Michigan: Biochemistry is required
- Mayo Medical School: Biochemistry is required
- Univ. of Minnesota – Minneapolis: Biochemistry is required. Genetics is recommended.
- Univ. of Mississippi: Biochemistry, genetics, vertebrate anatomy, and histology/physiology are recommended
- Saint Louis Univ.: Biochemistry is recommended

- Univ. of Missouri, Columbia: Biochemistry is recommended
- Creighton Univ.: Biochemistry and genetics are recommended
- Univ. of Nebraska: Biochemistry and genetics are required
- Univ. of Nevada: Biochemistry and genetics are recommended
- Dartmouth Univ.: Biochemistry is recommended
- Univ. of New Mexico: Biochemistry is required
- Albert Einstein College of Medicine: Biochemistry with lab is recommended
- Mount Sinai School of Medicine: Biochemistry and genetics are recommended
- New York Univ.: Biochemistry and genetics are recommended
- University at Buffalo School of Medicine: Biochemistry and genetics are recommended
- SUNY Downstate Medical Center: Biochemistry is recommended
- SUNY Upstate Medical University: Biochemistry and genetics are recommended
- Stony Brook University: Biochemistry is recommended
- Univ. of Rochester: Biochemistry, genetics w/lab, and anatomy/physiology w/lab are recommended
- Duke Univ.: Biochemistry is recommended
- Univ. of North Carolina, Chapel Hill: Biochemistry and genetics are recommended
- Univ. of North Dakota: Biochemistry is recommended
- Case Western Reserve Univ.: Biochemistry is recommended
- Northeastern Ohio Univ.: Biochemistry and genetics are recommended
- Ohio State Univ.: Biochemistry is recommended
- Univ. of Cincinnati: Biochemistry and genetics are recommended
- Wright State Univ.: Biochemistry is recommended
- Univ. of Oklahoma: Genetics is required
- Oregon Health Sciences Univ.: Biochemistry and genetics are required
- Drexel Univ.: Biochemistry and molecular biology are recommended
- Pennsylvania State Univ.: Genetics is recommended
- Univ. of Pennsylvania: Biochemistry and genetics are recommended
- Ponce School of Medicine: Biochemistry is recommended

- Universidad Central del Caribe: Biochemistry and genetics are recommended
- University of Puerto Rico: Biochemistry is recommended
- Brown Univ.: Biochemistry is required
- Univ. of South Carolina: Biochemistry is recommended
- Univ. of South Dakota: Biochemistry and genetics are recommended
- East Tennessee State Univ.: Biochemistry is required
- Texas A & M Univ. Health Science Center: Biochemistry is recommended
- Univ. of Texas – Medical School at Galveston: Biochemistry and genetics are recommended
- Univ. of Texas – Dallas Southwestern Medical School: Biochemistry is recommended
- Univ. of Utah: Biochemistry and genetics are recommended
- Univ. of Vermont: Biochemistry and genetics are recommended
- Univ. of Washington: Biochemistry is recommended.
- Marshall Univ.: Biochemistry is recommended
- Univ. of Wisconsin: Biochemistry is recommended

Taking the MCAT

What is the MCAT (Medical College Admission Test)?

The MCAT is a half day, standardized exam that tests your knowledge in a wide variety of subjects. The test is broken down into four sections. The first is Verbal Reasoning which is similar to the verbal portion of the SAT, except much more challenging. The second is Biological Sciences which covers biology courses and organic chemistry. The third is Physical Sciences which covers physics and general chemistry. The fourth is the Writing Sample which asks you to write an essay on two very broad statements.

Starting with the 2007 administration of the exam, the MCAT has been changed to a computer based format.

The MCAT is an half-day event at a testing center and takes 4 hours and 50 minutes to complete.

Testing starts at 8 AM, but you'll need to arrive early in order to register and be officially identified for security purposes. This actually takes a long time, so be prepared to wait. You'll want something to keep you occupied, though, because standing there stewing about the test won't do you any good. And I highly recommend headphones, because there's just something unsettling about a large group of people waiting nervously for their exam.

Time will seem to fly by while you're taking the test, but you'll still need to fight fatigue throughout the day. If you've taken some full-length exams in the weeks leading up to the exam through a review course or on your own, you'll have the necessary endurance, so please do this.

All sections, except the writing sample, which is essay, are multiple choice. Students are typically given a section of text to read and then asked questions about the section. Some unrelated (not related to the passages - to test some general knowledge) questions are also part of the exam, but are far less frequent than the passage-related questions.

There is not much time to read the passages and answer questions, so you have to work at a pretty fast pace. Considering the fact that you have to first read a passage before answering questions you may actually have less than 1 minute to answer each question. The questions are not easy and often require some thinking, reasoning and interpretation.

Each of the three multiple choice sections is worth 15 points for a total of 45 points, but it's nearly impossible to achieve a perfect score. The average MCAT score each year is somewhere around a 24 (8 in each section).

A good (competitive at most MD schools) score is around 30 and a stellar score is somewhere above a 34 to 36 (competitive at the top medical schools in the country). The writing sample is scored with a letter system from J (lowest) to T (highest), but is much less important than the number score. You never hear anyone mention the letter score. All you ever hear people talk about is the number, although some people insist that they are also considered in the admissions process somehow.

Taking the MCAT

Not to be dramatic, but the MCAT is probably one of the three most important tests you will ever take in your life (the other two? the SAT and the Medical Boards). However, the MCAT is unlike any other standardized test that you've taken before. It does not necessarily test how much you know, but how well you think. It relies a lot on comprehension skills and is also a bit of an endurance test. It is a long test and preparation for it will occupy a significant amount of your time.

The general format of the test doesn't change significantly from year to year. The test has four sections.

General Information about the MCAT

The MCAT heavily emphasizes reasoning and problem solving. Factual knowledge of the basic sciences is assessed primarily by your ability to solve problems. Quantitative assessment is incorporated into the two science sections. *Note: You are expected to know information from the introductory levels of the courses mentioned—the test does not presume advanced knowledge of science. However, people have found it helpful to have taken one additional year of upper division biology courses such as Genetics, Physiology and Biochemistry.*

To most people, the MCAT is the scariest part of the application process. Usually students take it during the spring or fall of their junior year, and they need to deal with their regular course-load at the same time with previewing for the MCAT.

The current MCAT's are designed to test not only your proficiency in the basic sciences, but also to test your general problem-solving, critical thinking, and communication skills developed in humanity curricula. Therefore, the Verbal reasoning section is added with variety a passages from many different educational fields.

Nearly all medical schools suggest that you take the MCAT in the spring of the year you apply so that you have a chance to apply for Early Decision Program (EDP). Moreover, in case you don't do well on the exam, you still have a chance to take it again.

The current MCAT's consist of four sections. The test lasts four hours and 50 minutes, but when you add the usual standardized testing delays, you'll be there a little longer. Ten minute breaks are given between each section. A ten minute tutorial is given at the beginning and a ten minute survey is given at the end. The following table summarizes the total number of questions, time, and score format for all four sections:

Section	Number of questions	Time (minutes)	Score
Verbal Reasoning	40	60	1-15
Physical Science	52	70	1-15
Essay Writing	2	60	J-T
Biological Science	52	70	1-15

Verbal Reasoning Section

This section involves multiple-choice questions based on reading passages about 500 words long. The topics are selected at random from humanities, social sciences, and natural sciences. However, you're not expected to have any knowledge of the subjects. The answers can be obtained or deduced from the passages.

People who usually do well on reading comprehension -- for example, those in English major -- don't get any trouble with this section at all. However, if you are a science major, the best way to deal with this section is to increase the amount of your reading. Newspaper editorials are the great source because their lengths, styles, and contents are similar to the passages on the MCAT.

This is very similar to the Verbal SAT section, but it is more difficult. The reading passages that they give you cover a broad range of topics and you need to be prepared for anything. Whatever you do, don't blow off studying for this just because it's a non-science section. Remember, this test is all about how you think, and that includes how you think about things that are not science related.

This section consists of passages followed by multiple choice questions. Usually there are several passages, each half a page long with questions pertaining to the passage following it. The total number of questions in this section is 40.

Physical Sciences:

This consists of physics and general chemistry questions. Unlike Verbal Reasoning section, you're expected to answer the questions based both on your knowledge of basic science concepts and your comprehension of the information presented in passages, graphs, and tables that accompany the questions. That is why you should review course materials in order to increase your score in this section.

You're given a periodic table of elements. Some of the problems give relevant formulas, others expect you to know relationships. The bottom line is that it is better to memorize formulas. Alternatively, you need at least to know how variables interact among themselves when one goes up what happens to others?

Writing Samples:

In the third section, you must write two essays (30 minutes each). Basically you need to write two essays each of which addresses a concern presented on a comment provided for each essay. You must construct three main tasks for each essay:

1. Interpret the statement: what the statement means to you.
2. Oppose the statement: Is there any case when the statement has some conflict?
3. Resolve the conflict

The key to this section is that the graders are only expecting "first-draft" effort. Therefore, try to finish all required tasks. Don't leave the essays incomplete just because you spend too much time in revising, rewriting, or polishing some statements or a part of the whole essay.

One thing to note, the essays can be on just about anything, but rest assured they will not be on anything related to science. That's what the other sections are for.

Biological Sciences:

This section has identical format with section two. However, its contents are based on biology and organic chemistry. Again, reviewing your old materials helps you a lot in this section.

One problem which you may get on this section is your fatigue after long struggling on other sections. A good solution for this problem is to bring a big power bar with you. During section three, eat the candy to power you up on the last section.

Many questions are not of the type you've seen on your exams. They require problem-solving and integration of more than one concept. You can only learn to solve them by practicing, so do sample exams.

Applied organic chemistry seems to be the emphasis. It tests you on skills and understanding. Knowing facts is not enough here, you need to learn to integrate them.

The Biology section covers all the topics you can imagine--hormones are big, so is genetics. It is helpful to take a class in human physiology in order to prepare for this one or at least read a human physiology book on your own.

What MCAT scores medical schools expect?

Just try to get all your MCAT scores as high as possible. Many schools look for consistency in MCAT scores. If your three numerical scores are above 10, and your essay score in above N, your chances of an interview are quite good. However, even if you get 14's in two science sections, but you get only 6 on your Verbal Reasoning, you may get in big trouble.

When do I take the test?

The MCAT should be completed in the spring of your junior year, or during the fall at the latest, otherwise, you will not be able to enter medical school directly after college. Both dates have their advantages and disadvantages. Taking the test in the spring allows you to obtain your scores early and begin the application process sooner; however, you may not have sufficient time to study for the test because of your college coursework. This lets you start your application sooner, and also lets you decide if you want to take the test over in the fall. However, you will be stuck studying for the test during the school year, on top of all of your other work. But if you are the type of person that can keep on top of things and manage to get in a couple hours of studying each week, this might be the better option.

Taking the test in the fall gives you more time to prepare, but your scores (needed to complete the application process) won't be available until later. If you do poorly on your first MCAT, do not retake until you have fully mastered the material. Medical schools believe that those students who have consistently poor grades on the MCAT will also do poorly on the USMLE (a national, standardized test given to medical school students which must be passed in order for graduation from medical school).

Doing it in the fall allows you more time to prepare for the test, since you can spend the majority of your summer free time studying; and, trust me, that is what you will be doing. However, you won't get your scores until some time in late fall, so you may not be able to complete the application until later on in the semester. But ultimately, it's up to you to decide which test would be best for you.

How do I prepare for the test?

You have three choices: (a) don't prepare and try to "wing" it, (b) go to the bookstore, get a MCAT study book, and prepare by yourself, or (c) take a Kaplan or Princeton type prep-class. *The first option* is certainly not recommended. The MCAT is a very difficult test—the majority (95%) of the questions are analytic, and tied to several paragraphs of introductory information/data/results. *The second option* is recommended for those who are diligent in their studies and already have a basic understanding of science material. Prep-books are usually 700-1000 pages long and **every page** is completely filled with crucial information; remember that the publishers are trying to cover all of organic chemistry, general chemistry, physics, biology, and reading comprehension in one book! If you want to do well, you should begin studying this material (3-6 hrs/wk) at least six months before the test.

For those who are able and willing to work through self-study, there are many good review books, including a Kaplan Comprehensive MCAT review book. They contain the same basic material used in the course, but you are on your own. So, you have to set aside a certain number of hours per week for a few months to review and work through the materials on your own.

I would highly recommend purchasing the real paper or web practice MCATs online (preferably the web versions since the MCAT is now computerized). They are the real deal, from the makers of the MCAT and not some version made up by Kaplan, Princeton Review or other test prep companies. They are well worth the money and you can take them under real testing conditions (set aside a few Saturdays at your library in a quiet corner, or at home - undisturbed). You get the actual test booklets and multiple choice answer sheets, or access to the online equivalent and you can grade yourself at the end to see how you did.

The third option is for those who think they need some basic assistance in studying, or for those who don't require basic assistance but want to score very high on the MCAT. Taking a prep-class means more time—NOT less—preparing for the MCAT. In addition to doing all of the necessary studying you must do in option #2, you have to go to prep-classes (6 hrs/wk), and take supplementary practice tests and quizzes (2 hrs/wk). If you take a prep-class and don't make use of the prep-classes or practice tests/quizzes, you will not do any better than if you studied on your own. The prep-courses are also expensive.

Often these are offered through Kaplan or Princeton. There are a few things to think about regarding these. First, they're expensive. Second, they take up a lot of time. Third, it was a lot of work. One of the most important things the courses teach you is the strategy for taking the MCATs. A lot of the instructors have taken the test, and they have been trained in how to teach people to take the MCAT. Once again, you have to decide which way is best for you.

So, you could say that you still have to put effort into the class like any other class you have taken before. Just attending the prep course may not help you out much, although they do cover a lot of test taking strategies which are helpful for test taking in general and not depending on how much material you learned. Also note that these courses work only for review. If you have not had Physics or Organic Chemistry before, don't think you could just learn the material in the prep course. These are review courses.

They also offer practice tests throughout the course and provide hints and tricks, do all kinds of analysis of what was on previous tests, etc. and help you with time management techniques and other topics. This type of review may be very well worth it if you are the type of person who is a procrastinator or needs a structured program that is already set up and scheduled.

There are actual full-length MCAT exams available directly from the company that administers MCAT.

Again, regardless of which option you decide to choose, you should begin studying 3-6 hrs/wk at least six months before the test.

You really have to be focused in order to get all of the material covered in time, and you have to be able to push yourself to understand the material. But it can be done successfully.

Since the MCAT is now in the computerized format, get access to these real tests online to take them under similar circumstances as you will with the real exam.

The MCAT is really a thinking test. You will need to know the sciences to do well, but many of the questions do not directly test knowledge. They may ask you to interpret some data or extract some answers from a passage. It has been said that you cannot really cram for the MCAT.

The MCAT Student Manual has extensive preparation materials, sample questions and full-length practice tests. If you are preparing on your own, be sure to purchase this book. There are also six additional practice tests available—you can order them through the AAMC.

At http://www.aamc.org/students/mcat/about/wsitems.htm you will find many MCAT writing sample prompts with essay instructions. Each writing sample will ask you to complete 3 tasks per essay. Make sure you read the instructions carefully. This prompt list contains samples which may appear or be very similar to the MCAT you will be taking this coming year.

Self-Study Resource Materials List:

1. **AAMC Materials** http://www.aamc.org/students/mcat/
   • **MCAT Student Manual,** which contains a working definition of each content term or area.
   • **Practice Tests: I, II, III, IV, V, VI**—Tests III-VI reflect most accurately what the test will really be like. The Verbal section of Test III is reported to be the most challenging. The most recent tests can either be purchased to take as an on-line computer exam or as written tests you can keep. Earlier exams I-III are only available in hard copy. Many of these tests along with a new Practice Test VII are available to take on-line after purchase.
   • Practice Test expanded answers optional (can be too detailed)
   • Practice Problems for Verbal, Physical and Biological Sections—these questions are a little different than the actual MCAT test questions used but can be helpful.
2. **Review Science Materials:** (you should only buy one - all preparation manuals have errors)
   • Complete Preparation for the MCAT-published currently by Lippincott (the

book originally written by Flowers).

- • Preparation for MCAT-Silver and Flowers
- • Kaplan MCAT Prep Materials—not as organized as the above two.
- • ExamKrackers Complete MCAT Study Package, 5th Edition by Jonathan Orsay

3. **Science Textbooks:**
- • One in each area of the sciences to review for specifics; far to detailed for general study

4. **Study Skills Materials:**
- • Problem Solving and Comprehension-Whimbey/Lochead (recommended highly)
- • Memory Aids-several books available; all are helpful
- • Time Management-several systems available to personalize schedules
- • For those students with weak backgrounds and poor standardized test taking skills use 10 SATs by the College Boards-(only covers math/verbal sections)

5. **General Reading:** To prepare for the verbal section you should be trying to read non-science materials at least one hour a day and up to two hours if you have particular problems with verbal standardized tests.
- • New York Times Book Review*
- • New York Review of Books*
- • Atlantic Monthly
- • Harpers
- • New Yorker
- • Wall Street Journal
- • Economist

  * Similar size articles to MCAT verbal section. They have a range of subject matter, and you should read them with a critical eye.

6. The MCAT does not test how well you calculate; many times numeric answers are rounded up. There is no scratch paper on the exam. Think back to your concept area when looking at the answers. Devote at least a course work's worth of time to preparation (3 hours of lecture + 4 hours of lab time + study time for

the course, 10-15 hours per week). Fine tune as you develop your work habits and figure out what works best for you.

7. **MCAT Test Taking Tips:** Some passages and questions can be termed reference questions where the answer can be read directly from the previous passage. Some questions are inference questions and no matter of rereading will give you the answer. Then there are free standing questions where you have no passages. Generally in multiple choice tests, try to eliminate at least two of the answers and if you can narrow it down to two-it is ok to guess. Unlike the SAT, you are not penalized for a wrong answer so guessing is favorable to leaving a question blank.

Registering for the MCAT

MCAT registration is done online. Be sure to apply well in advance of the deadlines. There are no exceptions made for missed deadlines. The registration form will give you the option of releasing your scores to your health professions advisor.

If you plan to apply for fee assistance, please go to the AAMC website (http://www.aamc.org/students/applying/fap/start.htm) to fill out a fee assistance application. AAMC must receive fee reduction applications usually by mid February. When you apply for a fee-assistance you are applying for both the MCAT registration and the AMCAS fee reductions for applying to medical school. It is important to get this done early because it takes them a long time to process.

If you are planning to request special accommodations during the MCAT, please see www.aamc.org/students/mcat/about/accommodations.htm. The MCAT program office must receive web requests no later than the late registration receipt deadline. If you cannot take a Saturday test, consult the MCAT instruction booklet for instructions on how to arrange a Sunday test.

Once you have sent in your MCAT registration, SAVE THE INSTRUCTION BOOKLET AND BE SURE TO TAKE IT WITH YOU TO THE TEST

Photographs

During the medical school application process you will be asked to provide numerous photos. Any current and valid government issued photo identification containing both a photo and a signature may be used for the MCAT. Typically, examinees bring their driver's license or passport. As you begin to receive secondary applications you will be asked to submit more photos; some schools will want you to bring photos to the interview. If you pay the standard price for passport photos can be as much as $8.00. You may want to try this alternative that brings the price per picture down to 20-30 cents:

1. Get a set of passport photos (2 pictures or so) from any standard passport photo location. Dress nicely for these pictures.
2. Take your photo to a well-established photocopying facility.
3. Ask to have a color copy of the photograph made and replicated (or pasted) to fill a single page. This way you can have your photograph copied up to 30 times on one page.
4. Ask for a several copies of this multiple image page on "hard stock" paper. These copies are about $4.00 each. The hard stock paper gives the image a "photograph-like" feel. I think you can also ask for photo quality paper.

A better quality option is to use a Kodak photocopier. These machines can be found at photo and camera shops. The multiple-image copy is on Kodak camera paper and the copies are nearly impossible to differentiate from photographs. The price per sheet is about $6.00 or about 50-60 cents per picture.

Also, you may be able to take your own picture with a digital camera and produce it in an appropriate program with a good quality color printer and photo quality paper.

On the Day of the Test

Get a good night of sleep before the exam. Take some high carbohydrate snacks for during the test. Relax and try to do your best. It is useless to try to study the morning of the exam. Don't do it, it just increases the level of stress.

Know how to get to the test site, where to park, etc. If necessary, make a dry run so that you will not be confused on the test day. Dress in layers so that you will be comfortable in any room temperature.

I would like to implore you, however, to make a point of remaining isolated and focused throughout much of the day. After each section of the MCAT is completed, people have a natural desire to talk about it with their fellow test-takers, as they would do after any other exam. By steering clear of this, you'll remain focused on putting forth *your* best effort, without worrying about trying to compete with the other people there. Obviously you're competing, but what good is it going to do you to hear that your buddy thinks he failed Verbal Reasoning? What's done is done, and you need to focus on preparing for the next section. Listening to other people talk about how their test is going, good or bad, is a waste of your time, it's distracting, and it causes you to worry about your own performance. I remember that my friends and I made hardly any mention of how the test was going. Test day is stressful enough, and besides, you'll have plenty of opportunities to discuss your performance later that night at your post-MCAT party.

Bring tissues, snacks and energy bars (just in case). Please keep in mind that food cannot be eaten during the exams. The snacks are for your breaks.

Once you have completed the test, it will be scored and those results will reside permanently in the AMCAS database. You cannot cancel those scores. The scores are reported to you and to other institutions or agencies only if you authorize them to be released. You would do this by marking yes on any one of a series of six release questions. Three of these questions are asked on your registration materials, and three are available on the day of the exam in the test center review questionnaire, you fill out at the end of the test.

Go out and celebrate afterwards to erase all that accumulated knowledge. I usually tell people not to take the MCATs again unless you think there was some reason you could get significantly better scores. Every time you take the test you will probably improve by 2 or 3 points your score, but that is expected since you are now very familiar with the format. You also risk bringing your score down which will not look good at all. Just try to do your best and after you are finished, don't fret about them anymore. MCATs are just one piece of information that med schools use to evaluate you, a low score won't necessarily eliminate you from consideration, conversely a high score will not guarantee you admission. Note though, that some schools use formulas with the MCATs and GPA to initially screen out applicants for interviews. You may want to ask schools you are interested in applying to whether they use one of these formulas. MCATs can help you make up for some low grades, but not completely. Your best bet is to concentrate on your whole package, not just on one element.

Examination tips during the exam:

- Read all directions with great care
- Time is a limiting factor, so don't leave a question blank, but give your best guess because you don't get any penalty for guessing
- Be conscious of your allotted time
- In the Verbal Reasoning section, quickly read the questions before you read the passage
- All questions in the Verbal Reasoning section are based only on information the passage. Don't use your own knowledge to answer the questions.
- Before starting each essay, think of a very brief outline
- While working the science sections, rely on your fundamental understanding of chemistry, biology, and physics.

You should never take an official MCAT as a practice. You can only take the exam three times. Medical schools regard taking multiple tests poorly.

How Do Schools Receive Your MCAT Scores?

AMCAS schools automatically receive your MCAT score; however, you must have them sent to non-AMCAS schools.

Should I retake the MCAT?

After you receive your scores you may wonder whether or not you should retake the exam. The answer is not just a matter of what you scored on the test.

Most medical schools do not advise taking the MCAT multiple times unless there is a serious reason why the scores on one test are not what you were expecting. If you really prepared for the test, and for sickness, or personal reasons or something else that is significant, your scores do not, in your opinion, represent your level of skill, then consider taking the test over again. However, if you did prepare adequately and just want to get a better score, it might not be the best idea to retake the test unless you know that you will significantly increase your scores. A lot of med schools will actually look down on someone who has taken the MCAT more than twice.

If you score low on the MCAT, it may be a good idea to retake it. However, you absolutely have to show improvement. I know some students who increased their scores a good 3-5 points and it made all the difference. If you score the same or lower than your original MCAT score, retaking the MCAT only hurts you because you have just demonstrated that you really cannot do it, even if you have another chance.

Often, it's advisable to take a prep course, if you haven't already done so, to prepare for retaking the MCAT, especially if you didn't take the exam seriously enough the first time. You have to be willing to put a lot of hard work into preparation before retaking the exam again - just retaking it will buy you nothing.

Sometimes, if the MCAT score is not very high, but still acceptable, it might be better to work on extra-curricular activities to increase the overall strength of the application to compensate. However, a lower MCAT can limit some of your medical school choices. Certain medical schools may not consider you at all. Generally speaking, DO and

Caribbean medical schools have lower MCAT requirements, and there is also quite a bit of variation between various MD schools.

So, the decision to retake the MCAT may depend on your goals overall and not necessarily on the score you received the first time. Also, keep in mind that it is very hard to increase your MCAT score, especially if you were prepared for the test the first time and there is not much else you can do to prepare. Increasing a score from a 24 to a 28 is probably much easier than raising a score from a 30 to a 34.

You need to ask yourself:

Can I do better?

> Some students feel that they were as prepared as they could have been the first time they took the test, and that even with more studying, they feel that they could not do better. Other students feel that they did not put enough time and effort into studying. If you feel like you can be much more prepared for the next test then it may be worth the time and effort (and money) you'd spend over the next two months to retake the test. It is important to note that in large populations of applicants who retake the MCAT after receiving 10's in each section, only half show an improvement in their scores. Consult your Pre-Health Advisor.

Is my score adequate?

> The national average total MCAT score of applicants admitted is about 30. However, each school has its own average. You should check the average score for each school to which you plan to apply. Keep in mind that averages are only guidelines. Just because you scored higher than average does not mean that you will be accepted and just because you scored below average does not mean you won't. To look at some important data collected by AMCAS on average retest performance go to
> http://www.aamc.org/students/mcat/scores/examineedata/tables.htm.

Are my grades adequate?

What is your GPA – overall and BCPM (science GPA calculated by AMCAS)? If you apply through AMCAS you can get a printout of how AMCAS calculates your GPA. If your GPA is lower than the averages of the schools to which you are applying, then ideally you would want an MCAT score higher than their averages. If your GPA is higher than the averages, then you may get away with an MCAT score slightly lower than their averages, although a higher MCAT score would of course be better.

Is the rest of my application adequate?

If you've got a lot of extracurricular activities, and you think your letters of evaluation are really strong, then these factors will add to the quality of your application. If you think these areas are weak, then you would want other factors (GPA, MCAT) to be as strong as possible.

How important is it to get accepted this year?

This seems like a stupid question. Obviously, if you are applying to medical school right now, you want to get in this time and not have to deal with reapplying next year, taking a year off school, etc. However, students do have different perspectives on this. Some students are extremely focused on getting into medical school as soon as possible and in doing absolutely everything that is humanly possible to make this first application as close to perfect as it can be. On the other hand, some students, while they of course want this application to be the best that it can be, are willing to risk applying "as-is" (with a good-but-could-be-better application) and worry about retaking the MCAT if they do not get accepted. This is something that you should discuss with your advisor.

GPA and MCAT Scores

Note that the two following tables give average GPA and MCAT scores for both allopathic (MD) and osteopathic (DO) schools for a few years.

Data for allopathic (MD) schools

Entering Year	Overall GPA	MCAT (Verbal)	MCAT (Phys)	MCAT (Bio)	MCAT (Essay)	MCAT Total
2004	3.62	9.7	9.9	10.3	P	29.9 P
2003	3.62	9.5	9.9	10.2	P	29.6 P
2002	3.61	9.5	10.0	10.2	P	29.7 P
2001	3.60	9.5	10.0	10.1	P	29.6 P
2000	3.60	9.5	10.0	10.2	P	29.7 P

Data for osteopathic (DO) schools

Entering Year	Science GPA	MCAT (Verbal)	MCAT (Phys)	MCAT (Bio)	MCAT (Essay)	MCAT Total
2003	3.45	8.07	7.99	8.51		24.57
2002	3.44	8.06	7.97	8.50		24.53
2001	3.43	8.10	8.08	8.54		24.72
2000	3.43	8.11	8.18	8.69		24.98
1999	3.43	8.22	8.29	8.77		25.28

Note that it is easier to get into osteopathic (DO) schools than allopathic schools (MD) by roughly 5 points on the MCAT and something like 0.15 points on the GPA.

Regarding GPA calculation, MD schools count every course grade earned even if you have retaken a course. If you earned a "C" in Organic Chemistry the first time, retook the course and earned an "A" later, they will count both grades for calculating your GPA. DO schools only count the retake grade ("A" in this example) and not the lower grade you earned the first time ("C" in this example).

Generally speaking, the average MCAT score for MD schools is around 30 and GPA lies around 3.6 to 3.7. For DO schools, the average MCAT score is around 25 and GPA around 3.4. Especially if your MCAT score and GPA are below these values, your extra-curricular activities weigh heavier in the admissions decision and can make the difference between getting an interview and no interview.

Also note that Caribbean medical schools typically do not have any MCAT requirements (with a few exceptions) and will accept lower GPA and MCAT scores than MD and DO medical schools.

Choosing to what medical schools to apply is a tricky subject that must be approached with due diligence because it is an important factor that can increase your chances of admissions.

Researching Schools

1. **How many medical schools are there?** There are 124 allopathic (MD) medical schools in the US, 3 in Puerto Rico, and 16 in Canada. There are also 19 osteopathic (DO) medical schools in the US.

2. **How many schools should I apply to?** Assuming you are an average applicant (i.e., GPA = 3.5 and MCAT = 27) your probability of being accepted to a *particular* medical school is 1-2%. The more schools you apply to, the better your chances of being accepted. If you are average, it is recommended that you apply to 10-15 schools. (If you are below average and still want to apply, 20+ schools is best.)

3. **Where should I apply?** You're the only person that can answer this question. In order to make an informed decision, you must do a significant amount of research on the medical schools. It is recommended that you purchase the Medical School Admission Requirements (MSAR) which provides a large amount of information on all medical schools—the information in this book comes from the medical schools themselves. The book can be purchased from most bookstores at a cost of ~$25.00.

To Which Medical Schools Should I Apply?

Check the admissions requirements of the schools you are considering. Occasionally schools have requirements beyond the regular premedical course work. You can plan to take the courses during the application year. Indicate your intentions on the Academic Record portion of the application by checking the box Current/Future.

Establish any limitations/constraints

Eliminate state schools unless you are a resident of that state, and eliminate schools serving special populations unless you qualify.

Determine whether you have strong geographical constraints or preferences that lead to the elimination of other schools.

Take a realistic look at your GPA and anticipated MCAT and focus on schools for which you are clearly qualified.

For more specific information about the various curriculums and specific courses at each school you may want to look at the AAMC, Curriculum Directory at http://services.aamc.org/currdir/start.cfm

Establish Criteria

Make a list of the parameters/criteria that are important to you:

geographical location: region of the country? urban vs. rural?

emphasis: clinical vs. research? range of clinical training opportunities available, e.g. public vs. private hospitals, size of hospitals, etc.

size: small vs. large school?

academic environment: reputation as a teaching institution? traditional vs. innovative curriculum? problem-based learning? grading system? cooperative vs. competitive atmosphere? access to patients?

reputation: prestige, selectivity

cost: tuition + fees; living expenses; financial aid available?

diversity: proportion of women, minorities; attitude toward non-traditional students?

housing: on campus vs. community?

student life: social opportunities; recreational/cultural; general level of student satisfaction?

Philosophy? Osteopathic vs. Allopathic

other features?

Summary and Analyses

Once you have chosen your criteria, it is useful to construct a table in which you list various medical schools and evaluate how they compare with regard to the criteria you have chosen. Specific information about medical schools can be found in the AAMC publication: "Medical School Admission Requirements," the Princeton Review book: "The Best Medical Schools," and various other publications available in your Pre-health office.

You should plan to apply to 15-20 medical schools. Of these, a few could be your very top choices, whether or not you think they are within your grasp; the bulk should be schools for which you are clearly qualified and which you find desirable; and a few should be somewhat safer, less selective "insurance" schools. Remember, all schools will give you a fine medical education.

What should I look for in a school?

You should become familiar with a school's general information, curriculum, admissions requirements (pre-med. coursework), selection factors (GPA/MCAT scores), tuition, financial aid, application/acceptance policies, and reputation.

Where can I get all of this information?

The following web-sites should provide you with a great deal of information: (a) Association of American Medical Colleges, (b) American Association of Colleges of Osteopathic Medicine, (c) American Medical Association, (d) Kaplan Medical, (e) National Institutes of Health, (f) National Library of Medicine, (g) Medical School Web Pages.

Narrowing Down Your List

I have done all of the research, but my list is still too long. How do I narrow my choices?

As we shall see later, due to time constraints, as well as money and effort, you should not apply to more than 25 medical schools. To narrow down your list of choices, compare (in greater detail) the schools' competitiveness, cost, organization of preclinical years, primary care/specialty focuses, innovative educational approaches (problem-based learning, etc.), student evaluation and grading, United States Medical Licensing Examination (USMLE) Policies, special programs and opportunities (international internships, etc.), affiliated teaching hospitals, geographic location, campus safety and housing, and proximity to family/friends.

How many should I apply to?

There are a couple of factors that will influence this: finances, travel accessibility, interest in the program. But what I can tell, from discussing this with some of the people on medical school admissions committees, is that a good average number these days is between 15-20 schools. This might sound like a lot, but consider the fact that for any one school, your average chance of being accepted is about1 to 2% (I know that sounds depressing, but don't get hung up on the statistics: just focus on getting yourself through the process).

A lot of the information that you will you to compile your first list of schools can be found in the *Medical School Admissions Requirements* (MSAR). If you want the most up-to-date version, you can order the book from the American Association of Medical Colleges' web site, **www.aamc.org.**

A good idea is to compile a list of maybe thirty or so schools that you might be interested in, by looking at the type of program, style of teaching, tuition, admissions requirements, etc., from the MSAR. Then you can either call the schools and ask for an admissions view book, or look up the information online.

Applying

Although it may seem that the process of actually applying to medical school is secondary to getting your work done right, there are still rules to be followed. I had several friends with strong GPAs and good MCAT scores who were forced to wait through the summer after their senior year of college, waiting to hear from medical schools, simply because they waited too long to finish their AMCAS application. Some eventually got in, others didn't. No matter the outcome, though, having to wait for months and months to find out their fate certainly wasn't fun.

The ideal route to medical school begins with the taking of the spring MCAT, so that you'll know your score by mid-June. If you are satisfied with your score, do not sit on that score; apply immediately.

If you aren't happy with your spring MCAT score, or if you decided to wait until fall to tackle the test, there are still things you can be doing to make sure your application doesn't end up at the bottom of a stack of hundreds. The AMCAS application takes some time; you need to write a thoughtful personal statement, include a list of activities, and fill in a good amount of personal information. This can all be done without an MCAT score in hand, and you can even submit your application without an MCAT score. Of course, schools won't make a decision about whether to interview you until your score arrives, but at least you'll have your foot in the door.

So, how are you to know where to apply without an MCAT score to point you toward the right schools? Many applicants adopt a wait-and-see attitude about their MCAT score, claiming that they won't know where they have a legitimate shot until they get their scores back. Really, though, unless you decided to show up on test day without preparing at all, this lack of certainty is a poor excuse for not grabbing the bull by the horns and getting that application turned in. Most test-takers take several practice exams before the real thing, and it is unlikely that their real scores will deviate much from their last couple of practice attempts. Sure, you could squeeze a few extra points out in the final week, or you could choke on test day and drop a few points, but the point is that you'll have a good enough feeling about where you were prior to test day, and how you fared on test day, to have a reasonable idea of how you scored.

It's easy to put off until tomorrow what could be done today, but, in applying to medical school, time is of the essence. Some schools have rolling admissions, others don't, but the truth is that your chances of getting an acceptance decline as the year progresses. By late springtime, applicants are interviewing for wait-list spots, which can be disheartening. And remember, this application process takes place during your *senior year of college!* If ever there were a time to cut loose and relax, this is it. Early application doesn't mean you'll necessarily get accepted right away, or even at all, but it really does help. Get all the hard work out of the way in the summer, and you'll avoid unnecessary stress in what should be the crowning glory of your undergraduate years.

The Primary (AMCAS) Application

AMCAS: Or How to Apply to Medical School

The American Medical College Application Service (AMCAS) is a nonprofit, centralized service which facilitates the process of applying to participating U.S. Medical Schools.

The AMCAS application is available on the Internet at www.aamc.org. Or by mail from:
AMCAS
Section for Student Services
Association of American Medical Colleges
2450 N Street NW, Suite 201
Washington, DC 20037-1130
(202) 828-0600

Schools that do not accept the AMCAS have their own individual applications. (*Note*: If you are interested in osteopathic schools, you must instead complete an AACOMAS Application.). You download software from a website, complete the application on your computer, save it to disk, and then send the disk to AMCAS/AACOMAS. The software for the AMCAS-E and AACOMAS-E can be downloaded.

What are the components of the AMCAS?

There are several components that you have to fill out. The first section is your Personal Information. This is the standard biographical section that all applications have. It asks you your address, contact info, state of residence, etc. The next section is Post-Secondary Experiences. This section lets you tell the schools what you have done either in college or the summers in between or after college. You have room for only 15 experiences, so pick the ones you enter wisely. Anything dealing with medically related fields is a good bet to put in, but if there is something else that means a lot to you, by all means put it in. Always list the information in descending order of priority. You have a little space to provide an explanation, but there is a strict space limit and you won't be able to move on if you don't adhere to it.

The next section is probably the most important part of your application: your Personal Statement. This is the first time anyone on the admissions committees will get a chance to see your personality, so take your time with this. This is a great way to show off who you are, so be creative. Admissions councilors read literally *thousands* of these each year, so anything that will make you stand out in a positive way is great. Have a lot of people proofread this. Don't be afraid of the red pen. If people offer you advice on how to make something sound better, take their advice in stride. They don't want to hurt your feelings; they're just trying to make you look as good as possible. That said, don't try to change your whole essay to fit all of the criticisms. If you read it over and it says exactly what you want it to say, and it explains why you want to be a doctor, chances are you're done. Make sure that it is grammatically perfect, though. There's nothing worse than being rejected for a misplaced semicolon! NOTE: When you enter your essay into the application, check it over very carefully. You may have to fix some punctuation, etc.

After the essay is the Educational Record. Here you have to list every college you have ever attended, and your high school as well. You also have to manually put in every single class you ever took in college and the grade you got. Be careful with this section, as the different classifications of the classes that AMCAS uses can get a bit tricky.

Finally, you have to list all of the schools that the AMCAS application will go to. Please note, the schools will NOT receive this information, only that their school was listed. One additional section comes after this. If you have ever been written up or received any type of disciplinary action at college, you have to list it. Be honest. There's nothing to be ashamed of, and as long as it is relatively minor, it will not affect your chances of admission.

When should I begin filling out my AMCAS Application?

The AMCAS becomes available in April for the class entering in the fall of the following year. AMCAS begins accepting applications on June 1. Before your application is complete, AMCAS must receive an official transcript from every college you have attended; AMCAS begins accepting transcripts on March 15. You can verify if AMCAS has received your materials via telephone. You should complete the AMCAS as early as possible, and submit it no later than mid-September (otherwise, you may miss the application deadline of some medical schools). Assuming you have correctly filled in all application information, it takes AMCAS about one month to process your application and send it to the medical schools. Medical schools differ in their deadlines for receiving the AMCAS; they require it by October 15, November 15, or December 15, depending on the school.

Why should I apply early?

First, medical schools require your AMCAS Application, MCAT scores, letters of recommendation (and sometimes other things) before they consider your application; if any of these materials is not sent, they won't even look at your application—so get your AMCAS in early. Second, most schools have a "rolling admissions system" in which those who apply first get the first interviews, and consequently, will be granted admission before other applicants. If you send in your application late, the school may have already accepted a large number of people, reducing your chances of getting in. Third (assuming you will get an interview), in the early interview season there are few people interviewing, whereas later in the season, you may find yourself as part of a herd of interviewees—the admissions committee will have less time to look at your application, and it will be harder to stick out of the crowd. Fourth, admissions committees usually meet once per month to review applications; if you submit your application early, it may be brought before the committee five or six times which increases your chances of getting in.

How much will all of this cost?

The cost is usually $150 for the first school listed, and then $30 to $40 for every school after that.

Finally, certify and submit your application. If you have made any mistakes, AMCAS will return the application to you to fix, so try to get it all right the first time to avoid delays. It should take a few weeks to get the information to the schools.

Non-AMCAS Schools: Write to non-AMCAS schools for applications; addresses are available on the web. Also, some applications are available on the web. You will have to arrange to have individual transcripts sent to all non-AMCAS schools. Schools which do not participate in AMCAS are: Brown, U of Missouri-Kansas City, , U of North Dakota and all Texas schools except for Baylor. If you are interested in applying to a non-AMCAS school you must contact the school directly to request an application. Non-AMCAS schools begin accepting applications on varying dates. We recommend sending in these applications no later than mid-August.

TMDSAS: Five of the Texas medical schools are part of the University of Texas and have their own centralized application. It is available at http://www.utsystem.edu/tmdsas.

ACOMAS: The osteopathic medical schools also use a centralized application— AACOMAS (American Association of Colleges of Osteopathic Medicine Application

Service.) The AACOMAS application is available online in the spring at (www.aacom.org).

Both AMCAS and AACOMAS will begin accepting applications around June 1. We recommend that you complete the AMCAS/ACCOMAS/and Texas Applications by **late June or early July** so as to take advantage of the rolling admissions process. Even if you will not take the MCAT until August, it is important to file your application early.

Check the admissions requirements of the schools you are considering.

Application Process

The application process for medical school is long and intense. It really begins much earlier than when you actually fill out the application to send to the schools. It includes completion of many pre-med requirements, meetings with your pre-med advisor and pre-med committee, taking the MCAT and doing well in all of your pre-med course work.

Most schools will review applications as they are submitted on a rolling basis and extend interviews and finally offer spots in their classes in the same way. This means that they fill their classes on a first-come-first-serve basis. At first, they may have 150 spots to offer. With each passing week, as the admissions committee meets and extends offers, fewer and fewer spots are available. At the same time, they receive more applications, so the competition goes up and the number of available spots goes down. This means that an early application is one sure way of having the best possible chances of getting in.

Note that for Caribbean schools, the timing issue is less critical since they usually admit students 3 times per year. So, this information applies primarily to US allopathic (MD) and osteopathic (DO) schools.

All admission requirements to US medical school must be completed prior to applying to medical school and before taking MCAT, since MCAT tests the knowledge covered in pre-med classes. The requirements are 1 year of each: Biology, Chemistry, Organic Chemistry, Physics, all labs and English.

Aside from applying to a straight MD program, you have the options to pursuing combined MD program with a second degree as Ph.D, JD (Law), MBA (Master of Business Administration) and Master of Public Health (MPH).

Next you must take MCAT. You must pre-register for MCAT well in advance, so plan ahead. To get fee reduction you need to apply at least 2 months before the exam date.

If you're planning to apply to medical school, ideally you should take MCAT no later than spring of that year. If you take the fall administration, you will be placed at a great competitive disadvantage. Medical schools have what is called rolling admissions, which means that they look at applications as they become complete and offer acceptances and rejections along the way.

Since medical schools do not get your fall MCAT scores until later and they do not look at your application until it is complete with MCAT scores, their class will be almost full by the time your application is complete and they look at it. Even if your qualifications are good you might end up rejected from the places that would have accepted you had your application been completed earlier. If your application (GPA, MCAT, etc) is less than stellar and depending on various other factors such as your state of residence, if you take the fall MCAT you might be better off waiting a year to apply.

In general you will apply to 10 to 20 schools which comes down to $350 minimum. On top of that each school to which you apply through AMCAS will send you an additional application, called secondary application. Medical schools charge you anywhere from $50 to $100 in processing fees for the secondary application, which means that if you apply only to ten schools you'll be down another $1000.

It is also possible to get fee waivers for AMCAS--they let you apply to ten schools without paying any fees. If you apply to more than 10 schools you get the first 10 free and pay normal fees for applying to other schools. Many medical schools also honor AMCAS fee waiver and let you send in the secondary application without paying the processing fee. Again, eligibility depends on your financial status and you must apply well before you send in the AMCAS since it takes a few weeks to process--which might mean your application would be delayed.

This is a good time to remind you that once you apply, getting things out fast is very important. Send the AMCAS application back as soon as possible. Secondaries will start coming to you in a month or two. Do not keep secondaries for too long--get them out of the door as soon as you can so that your application can be reviewed sooner. Of course, do not sacrifice quality either--don't send complete trash to medical schools. Haste makes waste but the slow are left behind.

Timing is Everything

One of the most important aspects of your application relates to timing. You can talk with many applicants who applied late because they took the later MCAT or they just procrastinated. You will hear loud and clear that they would recommend applying as early as possible. I strongly agree. Applying as early as possible, interviewing on the first day possible, etc. are HUGE advantages.

As already mentioned, as time passes with a rolling admissions process, which are in place in almost all schools, your chances of getting in decrease due to more and more spots being filled with students and more applicants still arriving to be considered. Besides this factor of increasing competition, there is also peace of mind when you have received an offer early. Let's consider each step of the application process in detail now, in light of timing.

Early (spring) MCAT

You should take the spring MCAT so you can get your scores back sooner. Taking the fall MCAT will put you behind in the application process since you don't receive your scores back until the middle of fall. Many people have already received interview invitations and some have already been extended offers. Most schools will not consider your application and do not offer interviews until your MCAT score is received.

Early Applications

Make sure you start working on your AMCAS (MD) and/or AACOMAS (DO) applications starting after the MCAT is out of the way. They make the online applications available sometime around May 1st or so. You should also start working on your personal statement right away. I would recommend submitting your completed applications (AMCAS and AACOMAS) within the first week after you receive your MCAT scores. I think it is critical to submit as early as possible.

Early Secondaries

Fill out secondary applications received from the schools immediately and try to return them within less than 7 days, ideally within 2 days along with the money and other information they require. Turn these around as fast as possible. Some secondaries are more involved than others and all cost money. Don't procrastinate. To obtain early interviews, turning these around quickly is a must!

Early Interviews

If you have done the previous 3 steps very speedily (spring MCAT, early application, fast turn-around of secondaries), you will have interview invitations very early and will have the opportunity to interview during the first few weeks of the interview cycle, maybe the first week or even the first day interviews begin. Try to pick the earliest day for interviewing they offer. Ideally, you want the first day available on their schedule to interview.

Early Offers

Most medical schools extend offers within 2-3 weeks. However, the time to get notified varies greatly from school to school.

Why the hurry?

You should know the answer to this question by now. Do yourself a favor and do things early. It's the one factor of your application you have complete control over - and it really pays off!

Waiting Around

I know people who either took the fall MCAT or took their sweet time submitting their application, secondaries, etc. They were still interviewing well into March and did not hear back until the end of the entire interview season. Also, as already explained, less spots are available as the medical schools tend to have rolling admissions. At the beginning, really all of the spots are free and they try to fill them more aggressively. So, people who are equally qualified have less of a chance to get in during January through April than if they had interviewed during October (or earlier if offered).

Early Decision Programs

Don't confuse this program with applying early - this is a separate admissions program and not really part of the regular admission process. Not all medical schools offer the Early Admissions Program.

So, this is how it works:

You can only apply to ONE medical school's Early Admission program. The school has to make a decision by October 1st and notify you of acceptance or rejection. If you are accepted, you are obligated to attend that particular school and cannot participate in the regular application cycle at any other schools. So, you have to be sure the school you apply to is really the school you want to attend since there is no changing your mind later.

There are also some huge draw-backs to the Early Admission program, as you might already guess, since you can only apply to ONE school. If you are not accepted, you have wasted valuable time to get your application submitted to the other medical schools. You are essentially in the same spot as if you had taken the fall MCAT.

Note that if you were rejected during the Early Decision Program, you can still apply to the same school through the regular admissions process. You may even get a spot in the class. The early decision program can be useful for very strong (exceptional) applicants or for candidates who have specifically been encouraged by the school to compete for early admissions. Generally speaking, if you are a strong enough applicant for a spot through the Early Admission Program, you will also get a spot in the class through the regular process.

Drawbacks:

Personally, I think the Early Decision Program only limits your choices and is not very useful. Especially if you apply early (not through the Early Decision Program), you can also get offers by the middle of October. Also, the timing issue is a HUGE disadvantage - putting you way behind in the admission process if you are rejected.

Fill out the application

You really want to start filling this out the summer before senior year because it takes a long time and you might not have that much free time once school rolls around. The application normally becomes available online around May of the year preceding the anticipated start date of the school, so it will be there during the summer. You have to print out a special form to give to the Registrar that has your AMCAS info on it, so as soon as you can access it, it's a good idea to get that going.

Secondary Applications

1. **What are secondary applications?** A secondary application is additional application materials (sent by an individual medical school) which must be completed and returned to them (usually within two weeks) to continue the application process.

2. **Who gets secondary applications?** Some medical schools send secondaries to all candidates who submit an AMCAS application, whereas other schools are more selective. Generally, 50-75% of the applicant pool gets a secondary. Some schools do not require secondaries at all.

3. **What do the secondaries entail?** They can vary from very demanding to easy. Generally, you are required to complete 3-4 additional essays on a wide range of topics, re-print your completed pre-medical coursework/grades, and provide more detailed biographical information. Remember that secondaries are very important in the application process—a poor secondary shows that you have little interest in the school and a stellar secondary demonstrates your enthusiasm for the school. If you want to make a good impression on the committee, you should spend a great deal of time on your secondary application (use a typewriter to fill-in the application).

4. **How much do secondaries cost?** Generally, you must pay $50-100 per secondary.

Pay VERY close attention to the deadlines for each school. You want to make sure that everything is in on time and ready to go. Most school will not even look at your application before it is totally complete; so make sure you get everything done.

Return secondary applications you receive promptly within no more than 1 week from the day you receive them. Fast turn-around is essential and shows you are committed and interested in the school. Ideally, they should be turned around within 2 days.

The earlier you return the secondary, the earlier the school will schedule an interview and the earlier you will be able to receive an offer.

After your secondaries are done and sent off, be prepared to wait. And wait. And wait some more. It will be a couple of weeks to hear from any of your schools about interviews, just because of the sheer number of applications they have to go through. Check their websites and see if there are any deadlines for when they will tell you. If it's been more than a month or two, there's nothing wrong about calling up and asking about the status of your application. Just don't overdo it. One call after two months is fine. Twenty calls after two weeks is bordering on psycho.

Typical Questions from Secondary Applications for Various Medical Schools

1. Describe yourself?
2. What areas of medicine are you interested in? Explain your reasons.
3. Describe experiences that you consider to be important in your career as a physician
4. If you have been out of school, describe your activities during that period.
5. Have you applied to us or other medical schools in the US previously? Give dates.
6. List your extracurricular activities
7. To continue processing of your application to our medical school please remit a check for $85. (You must provide your own envelope!).
8. If you have any comments you want to bring to the attention of our Admissions Committee, write them here.
9. Explain why you chose to apply to our medical school.
10. Describe any research experiences you have had. Commend on them.
11. Where do you see yourself in 10, 20, 50 years.

12. What are your long-term goals in becoming a physician?

13. When you think of apples, what color are the oranges?

14. What people and/or experiences have been most influential in your life?

15. List courses you have taken to fulfill prerequisites for admission at our Medical School

16. Describe (an) experience(s) or projects in which you take particular pride.

17. Describe a difficult situation or an obstacle that you encountered in your life and tell us how you dealt with it.

18. What sparked your interest in medicine?

19. Describe why you decided to become a physician.

20. Describe any academic difficulties you might have had and how you dealt with them.

21. Of all extracurricular activities you have done while in college which is most important to you? Why?

22. What life experiences or relationships contributed to your development as an individual? Corroborate with specific examples that show how your personal qualities make you fit to become an MD.

23. Describe any honors or awards you have received.

If you were to get acceptances to more than one medical school, how would you choose where to go?

School Considerations

Many students are very passionate about school choice and why they chose a specific school or school type. These overviews and comparisons of different schools are very brief and much more could be said about each school type. Moreover, many people differ widely in opinion about which school type is most preferable for their very own reasons.

Some of your decision about school choice may depend on how competitive your overall application is, but other factors such as location or prestige of a school may also weigh in.

Quick overview (MD,DO, Caribbean, International)

For most applicants, allopathic (MD) schools are the most desirable option if they can gain admission. Generally speaking, people consider schools to be in the following order from most desirable, prestigious, and competitive to less desirable, prestigious and competitive.

1. Allopathic (MD) schools in the US and Canada.
  - Hardest to get in to, considered "most desirable"
  - Competitive atmosphere, most prestigious.
  - Highest MCAT and GPA requirements
  - USMLE1 pass rate: 91%, USMLE2: 92%, USMLE3: 94% - for 2004 (from NBME Annual Report)

2. Osteopathic (DO) schools in the US.
  - You learn some unique skills beyond those taught at MD schools

- Equal to MD for all practical purposes

- Slightly easier admissions due to lower MCAT and GPA requirements

- USMLE1 pass rate: 69%, USMLE2: 76%, USMLE3: 93% - for 2004 (from NBME Annual Report)

- Most students take the COMLEX board exams instead of the USMLE exams

3. Caribbean and other international schools (non-US)

- Easiest admissions, harder to get US residency of your choice

- Least prestigious, some not accredited, some practice limitations

- Low (or no) MCAT and GPA requirements

- USMLE1 pass rate: 58%, USMLE2: 68%, USMLE3: 68% - for 2004 (from NBME Annual Report)

Selecting a School

There are certainly many factors involved when trying to decide which schools to apply to.

Before selecting medical schools to apply to, you need to figure out what is important to you. Not all of the areas or questions below are relevant or important to everyone. Make a list of what matters to you. Then use it to figure out which schools meet your needs.

Of course, often you cannot choose. Maybe, your MCAT or GPA are not competitive enough or you just don't get offers where you'd like to go.

Here is a list of some of some factors that you may want to consider when making a list of potential schools:

Academics

Is my MCAT competitive for MD, DO, Caribbean, etc.?

Is my GPA competitive?

Do I have extra-curricular activities, research, etc.?

Do I meet all "special" coursework and other requirements of the school?

Do I need to apply to many more schools since my MCAT & GPA are weak?

Does the school admit lots of out-of-state students?

Reputation and Rankings

Is the school Ivy League or top rated?

Does the school have top research or other awards?

Is the school known for the specialty I'm interested in?

Is the school research or clinically oriented and does it match my interests?

Location

Is the school where I am willing/happy to live?

Are beach, mountains, entertainment close by?

Close to or far away from relatives or to home?

Away from it all?

Safety of campus

Family

Parents, siblings around?

Suitable area for raising your own kids?

Good school & neighborhood?

Reasonable housing close to the school?

Costs

Tuition

Cost of living

Commuting

Instate vs. out-of-state tuition?

Other

Are all the 3rd and 4th year rotations done locally or do I have to travel all over the country?

What are USMLE scores/pass-rate like for the school?

Are there any aspects of school that are exceptional?

Applying to the right schools is important. Now, nobody is saying you shouldn't aim high, but you need to be realistic when applying to medical schools. The fact is, the more competitive the school, the higher they set the bar when deciding to whom they should grant those coveted interviews. If you aced your MCAT and you've amassed an impressive academic record, congratulations, the sky's the limit. If you've only got average numbers, though, you would be ill-advised to apply exclusively to the elite schools without a safety school. By all means, don't sell yourself short, but don't be foolish, either.

If you don't know this already, here's something to consider: Below the top twenty or so medical schools, the other hundred are all pretty comparable in quality, and that quality is very high. Unlike law schools and other graduate programs, there are no bad medical schools. Think about it: Could a medical school really get away with turning out less-than-competent doctors for very long? They're partially funded with federal money, for goodness' sake. America doesn't mess around when it comes to its physicians.

There are a number of things to consider when deciding where to apply, not the least of which is the fact that you'll be spending at least four years of your life in the surrounding area. Do you despise snow and cold winters? If so, Harvard might not be a great fit, despite its reputation. Remember, this is going to be your home for a while. Also, while there really aren't big differences between schools as far as specialty is concerned, there are definitely schools that focus on primary care more than others. If you want to specialize in something after medical school, take a look at the school's reputation among residency directors, which is key for landing a spot in your desired specialty after medical school. And, if you can, try to match yourself with a school based on your learning style: Would you do better in a lecture-based curriculum, or one that uses problem-based learning? Small groups or large classrooms? Be sure you spend a good amount of time researching schools before you tie up time and money in the AMCAS and secondary applications.

Once you know where you *want* to go, look at the statistics and figure out if you have a reasonable chance of getting in. It would be wise to apply to a few "hit-and-hope" schools, some schools you feel relatively good about, and one or two safety schools. Just remember, these things cost money, both for AMCAS and for the secondary applications. Plane tickets also aren't cheap, and you'll have to interview at these places before they'll accept you. While the shotgun method of applying to medical school is certainly effective, it is also expensive.

For many students, there is one particular school (usually in-state) that they are particularly interested in attending. Some students will only apply to this school, or to schools higher in rank, on the logic that, "If I don't get in there, I'll just reapply, because I wouldn't want to go anywhere else." This may seem smart at the time, since applications cost money, but I would recommend still applying to one or two nearby safety schools, just in case your tastes change. I had friends who only applied to one school, and when that one school denied them admission, they were left facing a year in limbo. It would have at least been comforting to have the option of attending that less-desirable school (in their eyes), should they reconsider their earlier views and opt to just get their medical education underway.

Finally, it would be worth looking into whether or not your undergraduate university has special ties to any particular medical school. It may be that some schools are more welcoming of graduates of your alma mater based upon past experiences with particularly adept students, and having alumni in high places doesn't hurt, either.

Questions I Wish I Had Asked

Medical schools, like individuals are very different – in the philosophies, faculties, curricula, and the type of students they attract. Consequently, selecting the "best" medical school for your can be very challenging. The following set of questions was compiled by medical students from across the country to assist you in evaluating the schools you will visit: this list is by no means complete; it was designed to serve as a base for your own questions. Keep in mind that the interview represents a wonderful time for you to learn, so don't be shy about asking anyone your questions. Congratulations on your career choice and good luck with your interviews.

1. Are there any special programs for which this medical school is noted?

Curriculum

2. Describe this school's curriculum in the pre-clinical and clinical years. Are there any innovations, like Problem-Based Learning?

3. Are there opportunities for students to design, conduct, and publish their own research?

4. Is there a note-taking service? If they do you may want to know if it is University-run or student-run?

5. Is there flexibility in the coursework (the number of electives) and the timing of the courses (accelerating, decelerating, and time-off) during the pre-clinical and clinical years?

6. Has this medical school, or any of its clinical departments, been on probation or had its accreditation revoked?

7. How do students from this medical school perform on the USMLE? How does the school assist students who do not pass?

Evaluations

8. How are students evaluated academically? How are the clinical evaluations performed?

9. Is there a formal mechanism in place for students to evaluate their professors and attending physicians? What changes have been made recently as a result of this feedback?

Counseling/Student Support

10. What kind of academic, personal, financial, and career counseling is available to students? Are these services also offered to their spouses and dependents/children?

11. Is there a mentor/advisor system? Who are the advisors – faculty members, other students, or both?

12. How diverse is the student body? Are there support services or organizations for ethnic minorities and women?

Facilities

13. Tell me about the library and extra-curricular facilities (i.e. housing and athletic/recreational facilities).

14. Are there computer facilities available to students? Are they integrated into the curriculum/learning?

15. What type of clinical sites – ambulatory, private preceptors, private hospitals, rural settings – are available or required for clerkships?

16. Is a car necessary for clinical rotations? Is parking a problem?

Financial Aid

17. What is the current tuition and fees? Is this expected to increase yearly? If so, at what rate?

18. Are there stable levels of federal financial aid and substantial amounts of university/medical school endowment aid available to students?

19. Are there students who have an "unmet need" factor in their budget? If so, where do these students come up with the extra funds?

20. Are spouses and dependents/children covered in a student's budget?

21. Is someone available to assist students with budgeting and financial planning?

22. Does this school provide guidance to its students and to its graduates/alumni, on debt management?

Student Involvement

23. What medical school committees (e.g., curriculum committee) have student representation?

24. Are students involved in (required or voluntary) community service?

25. How active is Student Council/Government? Are there other student organizations?

Policies

26. Is there an established protocol for dealing with student exposure to infectious diseases?

27. Does this school provide, or does the student pay for, vaccinations against Hepatitis B or prophylactic AZT treatment in case of a needle-stick or accident?

28. Is there a school Honor Code? Is there a grievance process/procedure?

Residency

29. May I see a list of residence programs to which this school's recent graduates were accepted?

Questions to Ask Yourself

30. Does this school have strengths in the type of medicine (primary versus specialized care, urban versus rural practice environment, academic medicine versus private practice) that I will want to practice?

31. Would I be happy at this school (for at least the next four years)?

Choosing Schools

Schools of allopathic medicine award the M.D. degree. Allopathic medicine is defined as treating disease through drugs and surgery with a special concern for preventative medicine and public health. Schools of osteopathic medicine award the D.O. degree. Osteopathic medicine differs from allopathic in that the D.O. also incorporates manipulative (using the hands) procedures to treat parts of the body which are stressed or distorted. In practice, there is no difference in the functions performed by M.D.'s and D.O.'s. Both can prescribe medication, work in the full range of medical settings, and perform surgery with the appropriate training.

Historically, allopathic medical schools have enjoyed more prestige and have had slightly more stringent admissions requirements. However, osteopathic schools are also rapidly becoming more selective as their applicant pools grow. There is no need to limit yourself to applications to one type of school unless you are absolutely committed to a particular type of training. Be sure you know the difference between these two approaches before you apply.

Whether you are applying to allopathic schools, osteopathic schools, or both, you should apply to your state schools first. Because state schools benefit from state taxes, there is a strong preference to admit students who are residents. Not only are your chances better in the state in which you are a resident, but your chances are that much worse in applying to a state school of a state where you do not reside.

Transcripts

Your transcripts should be sent to each school to which you are applying from each school you attended as an undergraduate. Usually you will need to give the Office of the Registrar a list of the addresses where they should send your transcript and pay a couple dollars for each. Begin this process in plenty of time so your transcripts will be sure to get there before the deadline. Usually, one month is sufficient, but checking with the Office of the Registrar will help clarify.

How many schools should you apply to?

Some statistic shows that, on average, you have to apply to 14 schools to gain successful admission to medical school. Having said that, I know some people who only applied to one medical school and got in. I also heard about one applicant who applied to 50 medical schools and received only one offer. Also note that some applicants apply and don't receive any offers. Often, it takes one or more re-application attempts over several years to finally gain admission to medical school.

Typically, if you are an average applicant, applying to around 12-15 medical schools is advised. If you are a very strong applicant, applying to 3-5 medical schools may be sufficient. If you are a weaker than average applicant, you may want to apply to 20 schools or more. Err on the safe side. Apply to more schools than you need rather than not enough.

Sitting around for a year is no fun. You could be studying medicine.

Medical school admission is very competitive. In general, a given medical school accepts about 1-2% of applicants. On the other hand, about 30% of applicants get into medical school in any given year. This discrepancy is easily explained by the fact that virtually all applicants apply to at the very least ten medical schools.

In general, the more schools that you can apply to, the better. There are a number of limitations that may or may not apply to you and that will determine both to how many and to what schools you apply. These limiting factors arise from (1) your state residence and (2) your financial situation--to how many schools you can afford to apply.

In general, everyone can apply to private medical schools. But even many private schools have strong preference for in-state residents. So if you're applying to a private school outside of your home state, find out both its policies and actual statistics with respect to out-of-state applicants. If you're an international student, you must be even more careful and find out if they accept international students, especially if you did your premedical education outside of the US.

You should definitely apply to all your state's public medical schools. Almost all of them give very strong preference to in-state residents and many do not even accept out-of-state residents. On the other hand, you should not apply haphazardly to out-of-your-state public schools unless you ascertain that they accept out-of-state applicants---you would waste your money and precious time and energy that could be used to apply to schools where you actually have some chance of getting in. You can find this statistics in the AAMC's publication: Medical School Admission Requirements.

In general it is advantageous to apply to as many schools as possible, but of course the costs run up quickly. In addition, if you're applying to many schools you should plan to spend a lot of time filling out secondary applications--so plan ahead.

Even if your qualifications are impeccable, I still would recommend that you apply to 15 schools or so since there is much uncertainty when it comes to admissions. Should you get more than one acceptance, you will have a choice of where to go--which is a desirable bonus to get.

When deciding to what schools to apply, you should select schools that will accept you at least in principle as I discussed above. So if you're a Nevada resident do not apply to state schools in NY. There are a number of schools that have big medical school classes, i.e. over 150 students and those that do not have any in-state applicants such as the schools that are in Washington DC. You may want to consider applying there along with other places.

It should be obvious that you should apply to a range of schools from the most competitive to the least competitive to spread your risks.

Allopathic (MD) and Osteopathic (DO) school applications

The AMCAS application for allopathic (MD) and the AACOMAS application for osteopathic (DO) schools are quite lengthy and require some time and effort to complete. Don't think you can finish them in one day. But, you probably won't need weeks, either.

As already mentioned, you should have your application ready for submission within a week or so after receiving your MCAT scores back if you took the spring MCAT. If you took the fall MCAT, you don't want to wait until you have your MCAT scores back. You need to submit your applications during the summer, before or after you take the MCAT. Just realize that most schools will not even look at your application further until the MCAT scores are received. When you receive your scores, they are released to the medical schools you have applied to, the schools then complete your file and make decisions about extending interview invitations.

Both (AMCAS and AACOMAS) applications ask you for the following information:

1. Personal, contact and biographical information

2. Education background including high school and all colleges/universities, degrees, etc.

3. All college courses ever completed by type, course number, name, grade earned

4. Any special tests completed with scores (MCAT, SAT, ACT and others if applicable)

5. Experiences, including work, extra-curricular activities

6. Personal Statement/Comment

7. List of schools you wish to apply to

Note also that the MCAT scores are automatically released to AMCAS, but NOT to AACOMAS. You have to actually release your MCAT scores to AACOMAS on the MCAT Testing History System if you are applying to osteopathic (DO) schools.

If you fill out the AMCAS application (MD) first, then the AACOMAS application (DO) is easier to fill out since the latter requires shorter answers and explanations on everything, including the personal statement. So, I would recommend starting with the AMCAS application (print it out), then fill in the AACOMAS application if you plan to apply to both MD and DO schools.

Categories of Medical Schools:

- To easily decide what schools you should apply for, you may want to divide the number of schools you plan to apply into quarters and rank them on their relative appeals.
- The first quarter should include schools where you never expect to get accepted but would attend instantly if you did.
- The second quarter should include the very competitive schools .
- The third quarter includes strong (competitive) schools .
- And the final quarter includes all the rest.

When applying, you should take equal portions from each quarter. This will help increasing the odds of acceptance and maybe giving some nice surprises. You should also read the statistics on acceptance rate for each school in the AAMC's "Medical School Admission Requirements."

Some other questions you should consider in deciding which schools to apply for are:

- Do you like the location of the schools?
- What are the clinical and research facilities like?
- How is the education delivered?
- What about housing and health benefits?

When getting a decision of how many schools you should apply for, don't let financial matter interfere you although the expense for application for many schools can be trivial. Remember that $1,000-5,000 expense for you applications is not much in comparison to your total expense in medical school ($60,000-100,000 or even more). So, if you are a strong student, you should apply to no fewer than ten schools. And in general, it is good idea to apply for 20 or even 30 schools. The larger number of school you apply, the greater acceptance chance you have.

Choosing Your Future Medical Alma Mater:

Hopefully by the end of this process you'll have several letters of acceptance and be faced with the pleasant choice of finding your future medical alma mater. One of the first things to do is to look at financial matters. What kind of financial aid are they offering you and how much debt will you come out with after four years? This should be in the back of your mind, but not the deciding factor (unless your a California resident and accepted into a CA school, in which case you should go for it unless you get into a top-notch school). Think about the academic caliber of the schools you get into, the surrounding environment and the things you've heard from the students already

there. You may want to visit your top two choices again if you can and
talk to as many students and faculty as you can. You may even be able
to sit in a class or two.

M.D./Ph.D.

For those of you who want to aid mankind primarily by furthering our knowledge of
medicine, the M.D./Ph.D programs offered by a number of medical schools might be a
good fit. Students who pursue these degrees often aspire to work as faculty at medical
schools, or as researchers at places like the NIH. The program is a lot of work, I'm told,
but if this sounds like something you'd like to do, a life of research can be very
rewarding.

If you're seriously considering pursuing M.D./Ph.D., you will need to look at the
programs offered by the different medical schools across the country - not all programs
are offered at every school. Popular choices for the Ph.D. are things like pharmacology,
immunology, biochemistry, genetics, and cell biology, to name a few.

School	Tuition	Qualif	Scores
A,T. Still University of Health Sciences/ Kirksville College of Osteopathic Medicine (ATSU/KCOM) Kirksville, MO, USA Private DO school	I: $32390 O: $32390 for 2004	Degree: No MCAT: Yes	GPA: MCAT: 25
Albany Medical College Albany, NY, USA Private MD school	I: $39637 O: $39637 for 2005	Degree: No MCAT: Yes	GPA: 3.5 MCAT: 29.4
Albert Einstein College of Medicine of Yeshiva University Bronx, NY, USA Private MD school	I: $37550 O: $37550 for 2005	Degree: No MCAT: Yes	GPA: 3.67 MCAT: 31
Arizona College of Osteopathic Medicine of Midwestern University (AZCOM) Glendale, AZ, USA Private DO school	I: $30115 O: $35751 for 2004	Degree: No MCAT: Yes	GPA: MCAT: 26.4
Baylor College of Medicine Houston, TX, USA Private MD school	I: $6550 O: $19650 for 2005	Degree: Yes MCAT: Yes	GPA: 3.76 MCAT: 34.3
Boston University School of Medicine Boston, MA, USA	I: $39510 O: $39510	Degree: Yes MCAT: Yes	GPA: 3.5 29.4

School	Tuition	Degree / MCAT	GPA / MCAT
Private MD school	for 2005		MCAT:
Brody School of Medicine at East Carolina University Greenville, NC, USA Public MD school	I: $6034 O: $31024 for 2005	Degree: No MCAT: Yes	GPA: 3.6 MCAT: 26.1
Brown Medical School Providence, RI, USA Private MD school	I: $34472 O: $34472 for 2005	Degree: No MCAT: Yes	GPA: 3.6 MCAT: 31
Case Western Reserve University School of Medicine Cleveland, OH, USA Private MD school	I: $37944 O: $37944 for 2005	Degree: Yes MCAT: Yes	GPA: 3.6 MCAT: 31.8
Chicago College of Osteopathic Medicine of Midwestern University (CCOM) Downers Grove, IL, USA Private DO school	I: $29050 O: $29050 for 2004	Degree: No MCAT: Yes	GPA: MCAT: 25.8
Chicago Medical School at Rosalind Franklin U-Med & Sci North Chicago, IL, USA Private MD school	I: $36740 O: $36740 for 2005	Degree: Yes MCAT: Yes	GPA: 3.42 MCAT:
Cleveland Clinic Lerner College of Medicine of Case Western University Cleveland, OH, USA MD school		Degree: Yes MCAT: Yes	
Columbia University College of Physicians and Surgeons New York, NY, USA Private MD school	I: $38720 O: $38720 for 2005	Degree: No MCAT: Yes	GPA: 3.79 MCAT: 35
Creighton University School of Medicine Omaha, NE, USA Private MD school	I: $37519 O: $37519 for 2005	Degree: No MCAT: Yes	GPA: 3.65 MCAT: 28.8
Dartmouth Medical School Hanover, NH, USA Private MD school	I: $34500 O: $34500 for 2005	Degree: No MCAT: Yes	GPA: 3.65 MCAT: 31.2
David Geffen School of Medicine at UCLA Los Angeles, CA, USA Public MD school	I: $0 O: $12245 for 2005	Degree: Yes MCAT: Yes	GPA: 3.7 MCAT: 32.1
Des Moines University -- College of Osteopathic Medicine (DMU/COM) Des Moines, IA, USA Private DO school	I: $33307 O: $33307 for 2004	Degree: Yes MCAT: Yes	GPA: MCAT: 25
Drexel University College of Medicine Philadelphia, PA, USA Private MD school	I: $36770 O: $36770 for 2005	Degree: Yes MCAT: Yes	GPA: 3.43 MCAT: 29
Duke University School of Medicine Durham, NC, USA Private MD school	I: $34842 O: $34842 for 2005	Degree: No MCAT: Yes	GPA: 3.75 MCAT: 35.4
East Tennessee State University James H. Quillen College of Medicine Johnson City, TN, USA Public MD school	I: $17462 O: $35594 for 2005	Degree: No MCAT: Yes	GPA: 3.5 MCAT: 27.7

Eastern Virginia Medical School
Norfolk, VA, USA
Private MD school

I: $20521 Degree: Yes GPA: 3.41
O: $37933 MCAT: Yes MCAT: 30
for 2005

Emory University School of Medicine
Atlanta, GA, USA
Private MD school

I: $36000 Degree: No   GPA: 3.75
O: $36000 MCAT: Yes MCAT: 32.9
for 2005

Florida State U College of Medicine
Tallahassee, FL, USA
Public MD school

I: $17555 Degree: Yes GPA: 3.62
O: $47079 MCAT: Yes MCAT: 26.7
for 2005

George Washington University School of Medicine and
Health Sciences
Washington, DC, USA
Private MD school

I: $41193 Degree: No   GPA: 3.55
O: $41193 MCAT: Yes MCAT: 28.2
for 2005

Georgetown University School of Medicine
Washington, DC, USA
Private MD school

I: $37121 Degree: No   GPA: 3.61
O: $37121 MCAT: Yes MCAT: 31.2
for 2005

Harvard Medical School
Boston, MA, USA
Private MD school

I: $35800 Degree: Yes GPA: 3.8
O: $35800 MCAT: Yes MCAT: 34
for 2005

Howard University College of Medicine
Washington, DC, USA
Private MD school

I: $22695 Degree: No
O: $22695 MCAT: Yes
for 2005

Indiana University School of Medicine
Indianapolis, IN, USA
Public MD school

I: $20864 Degree: No   GPA: 3.66
O: $40549 MCAT: Yes MCAT: 29
for 2005

Jefferson Medical College of Thomas Jefferson University
Philadelphia, PA, USA
Private MD school

I: $38316 Degree: Yes GPA: 3.51
O: $38316 MCAT: Yes MCAT: 30.9
for 2005

Joan & Sanford I. Weill Medical College of Cornell
University
New York, NY, USA
Private MD school

I: $32320 Degree: No   GPA: 3.73
O: $32320 MCAT: Yes MCAT: 34
for 2005

Joan C. Edwards School of Medicine at Marshall University
Huntington, WV, USA
Public MD school

I: $14610 Degree: Yes GPA: 3.5
O: $38000 MCAT: Yes MCAT: 27
for 2005

Johns Hopkins University School of Medicine
Baltimore, MD, USA
Private MD school

I: $32200 Degree: Yes GPA: 3.86
O: $32200 MCAT: Yes MCAT: 34
for 2005

Kansas City University of Medicine and Biosciences
(KCUMB)
Kansas City, MO, USA
Private DO school

I: $33247 Degree: No   GPA:
O: $33247 MCAT: Yes MCAT: 24.5
for 2004

Keck School of Medicine of the University of Southern
California
Los Angeles, CA, USA
Private MD school

I: $39198 Degree: Yes GPA: 3.62
O: $39198 MCAT: Yes MCAT: 33.4
for 2005

Lake Erie College of Osteopathic Medicine (LECOM) Erie, PA, USA Private DO school	I: $24875 O: $25875 for 2004	Degree: Yes MCAT: Yes	GPA: MCAT: 23
LECOM - Bradenton Campus Bradenton, FL, USA Private DO school			GPA: 3.7 MCAT:
Loma Linda University School of Medicine Loma Linda, CA, USA Private MD school	I: $31692 O: $31692 for 2005	Degree: No MCAT: Yes	GPA: 3.69 MCAT: 29
Louisiana State University School of Medicine in New Orleans New Orleans, LA, USA Public MD school	I: $11186 O: $25333 for 2004	Degree: Yes MCAT: Yes	GPA: 3.6 MCAT: 28
Louisiana State University School of Medicine in Shreveport Shreveport, LA, USA Public MD school	I: $9776 O: $23924 for 2005	Degree: No MCAT: Yes	GPA: 3.7 MCAT: 28
Loyola University Chicago Stritch School of Medicine Maywood, IL, USA Private MD school	I: $34500 O: $34500 for 2005	Degree: Yes MCAT: Yes	GPA: 3.62 MCAT: 29.4
Mayo Medical School Rochester, MN, USA Private MD school	I: $24500 O: $24500 for 2005	Degree: Yes MCAT: Yes	GPA: 3.78 MCAT: 32.7
Medical College of Georgia School of Medicine Augusta, GA, USA Public MD school	I: $11850 O: $30976 for 2005	Degree: No MCAT: Yes	
Medical College of Wisconsin Milwaukee, WI, USA Private MD school	I: $28503 O: $33370 for 2005	Degree: Yes MCAT: Yes	GPA: 3.7 MCAT: 30
Medical University of Ohio at Toledo Toledo, OH, USA Public MD school	I: $19350 O: $47610 for 2005	Degree: Yes MCAT: Yes	GPA: 3.6 MCAT: 29.1
Medical University of South Carolina College of Medicine Charleston, SC, USA Public MD school	I: $6049 O: $42101 for 2005	Degree: Yes MCAT: Yes	GPA: 3.53 MCAT: 28
Meharry Medical College Nashville, TN, USA Private MD school	I: $27143 O: $27143 for 2005	Degree: Yes MCAT: Yes	
Mercer University School of Medicine Macon, GA, USA Private MD school	I: $30220 O: $0 for 2005	Degree: No MCAT: Yes	GPA: 3.58 MCAT: 25.1
Michigan State University College of Human Medicine East Lansing, MI, USA Public MD school	I: $22377 O: $50277 for 2005	Degree: Yes MCAT: Yes	
Michigan State University College of Osteopathic Medicine (MSUCOM) East Lansing, MI, USA Public DO school	I: $21306 O: $45106 for 2004	Degree: No MCAT: Yes	GPA: MCAT: 25

Morehouse School of Medicine
Atlanta, GA, USA
Private MD school

I: $24000 Degree: Yes GPA: 3.63
O: $24000 MCAT: Yes MCAT: 27
for 2005

Mount Sinai School of Medicine of New York University
New York, NY, USA
Private MD school

I: $33250 Degree: No GPA: 3.66
O: $33250 MCAT: Yes MCAT: 32.49
for 2005

New York College of Osteopathic Medicine of New York
Institute of Technology (NYCOM)
Old Westbury, NY, USA
Private DO school

I: $34447 Degree: Yes GPA:
O: $34447 MCAT: Yes MCAT: 23.7
for 2004

New York Medical College
Valhalla, NY, USA
Private MD school

I: $37200 Degree: Yes GPA: 3.5
O: $37500 MCAT: Yes MCAT: 30
for 2005

New York University School of Medicine
New York, NY, USA
Private MD school

I: $30625 Degree: No GPA: 3.7
O: $30625 MCAT: Yes MCAT: 33
for 2005

Northeastern Ohio Universities College of Medicine
Rootstown, OH, USA
Public MD school

I: $23307 Degree: No GPA: 3.62
O: $46614 MCAT: Yes MCAT: 26.4
for 2005

Northwestern University, The Feinberg School of Medicine
Chicago, IL, USA
Private MD school

I: $37308 Degree: No GPA: 3.69
O: $37308 MCAT: Yes MCAT: 32.2
for 2005

Nova Southeastern University College of Osteopathic
Medicine (NSUCOM)
Ft. Lauderdale, FL, USA
Private DO school

I: $23527 Degree: No GPA: 3.5
O: $29618 MCAT: Yes MCAT: 24
for 2004

Ohio State University College of Medicine and Public Health
Columbus, OH, USA
Public MD school

I: $22833 Degree: Yes GPA: 3.65
O: $35664 MCAT: Yes MCAT: 31
for 2005

Ohio University College of Osteopathic Medicine (OU-COM)
Athens, OH, USA
Public DO school

I: $21591 Degree: Yes GPA:
O: $30489 MCAT: Yes MCAT: 24
for 2004

Oklahoma State University Center for Health Sciences -
College of Osteopathic Medicine (OSUCOM)
Tulsa, OK, USA
Public DO school

I: $15743 Degree: No GPA: 3.5
O: $30892 MCAT: Yes MCAT: 26
for 2004

Oregon Health & Science University School of Medicine
Portland, OR, USA
Public MD school

I: $24100 Degree: Yes GPA: 3.65
O: $34101 MCAT: Yes MCAT: 31
for 2005

PCOM-Atlanta Campus
Gwinett County, GA, USA
Private DO school

Pennsylvania State University College of Medicine
Hershey, PA, USA
Public MD school

I: $29280 Degree: Yes GPA: 3.65
O: $40706 MCAT: Yes MCAT: 28.31
for 2005

Philadelphia College of Osteopathic Medicine (PCOM)
Philadelphia, PA, USA
Private DO school

I: $32859 Degree: Yes GPA: 3.4
O: $32859 MCAT: Yes MCAT: 24.5
for 2004

Pikeville College School of Osteopathic Medicine (PCSOM) Pikeville, KY, USA Private DO school	I: $27000 O: $27000 for 2004	Degree: No MCAT: Yes	GPA: MCAT: 22.5
Ponce School of Medicine Ponce, Puerto Rico Private MD school	I: $17836 O: $26590 for 2005	Degree: No MCAT: Yes	GPA: 3.4 MCAT: 21.3
Rush Medical College of Rush University Medical Center Chicago, IL, USA Private MD school	I: $39024 O: $39024 for 2005	Degree: No MCAT: Yes	GPA: 3.5 MCAT: 30
Saint Louis University School of Medicine St. Louis, MO, USA Private MD school	I: $38960 O: $38960 for 2005	Degree: No MCAT: Yes	GPA: 3.61 MCAT: 30
Southern Illinois University School of Medicine Springfield, IL, USA Public MD school	I: $18312 O: $54936 for 2005	Degree: No MCAT: Yes	GPA: 3.46 MCAT: 28
Stanford University School of Medicine Stanford, CA, USA Private MD school	I: $38295 O: $38295 for 2005	Degree: Yes MCAT: Yes	GPA: 3.7 MCAT: 34
State University of New York Downstate Medical Center College of Medicine Brooklyn, NY, USA Public MD school	I: $18800 O: $33500 for 2005	Degree: No MCAT: Yes	GPA: 3.56 MCAT: 29.3
State University of New York Upstate Medical University Syracuse, NY, USA Public MD school	I: $18800 O: $33500 for 2005	Degree: No MCAT: Yes	GPA: 3.6 MCAT: 29.25
Stony Brook University Health Sciences Center School of Medicine Stony Brook, NY, USA Public MD school	I: $18800 O: $33500 for 2005	Degree: No MCAT: Yes	GPA: 3.65 MCAT: 31
Temple University School of Medicine Philadelphia, PA, USA Private MD school	I: $33730 O: $41310 for 2005	Degree: No MCAT: Yes	GPA: 3.5 MCAT: 29
Texas A & M University System Health Science Center College of Medicine College Station, TX, USA Public MD school	I: $7750 O: $20850 for 2005	Degree: No MCAT: Yes	GPA: 3.65 MCAT: 27
Texas Tech University Health Sciences Center School of Medicine Lubbock, TX, USA Public MD school	I: $9450 O: $22550 for 2005	Degree: Yes MCAT: Yes	GPA: 3.63 MCAT: 28.5
The Edward Via Virginia College of Osteopathic Medicine (VCOM) Blacksburg, VA, USA Private DO school	I: $29500 O: $29500 for 2004	Degree: No MCAT: Yes	GPA: MCAT: 24
Touro University College of Osteopathic Medicine (TUCOM-CA) Vallejo, CA, USA Private DO school	I: $31945 O: $31945 for 2004	Degree: Yes MCAT: Yes	GPA: 3.4 MCAT: 26
TUCOM-Nevada Campus Henderson, NV, USA			

Private DO school

Tufts University School of Medicine Boston, MA, USA Private MD school	I: $43014 O: $43014 for 2005	Degree: No MCAT: Yes	GPA: 3.52 MCAT: 30	
Tulane University School of Medicine New Orleans, LA, USA Private MD school	I: $38172 O: $38172 for 2005	Degree: No MCAT: Yes	GPA: 3.54 MCAT: 31	
UMDNJ--New Jersey Medical School Newark, NJ, USA Public MD school	I: $21390 O: $33472 for 2005	Degree: No MCAT: Yes	GPA: 3.5 MCAT: 29.48	
UMDNJ-Robert Wood Johnson Medical School Piscataway, NJ, USA Public MD school	I: $21390 O: $33472 for 2005	Degree: No MCAT: Yes	GPA: 3.63 MCAT:	
Uniformed Services U of the Health Sci F Edward Hebert SOM Bethesda, MD, USA Public MD school	I: $0 O: $0 for 2004	Degree: Yes MCAT: Yes	GPA: 3.53 MCAT: 28.2	
Univ of North Texas Health Science Center at Fort Worth/Texas College of Osteopathic Medicine at Ft Worth (UNTHSC/TCOM) Fort Worth,, TX, USA Public DO school	I: $10925 O: $24025 for 2004	Degree: No MCAT: Yes	GPA: MCAT: 26.4	
Universidad Central del Caribe School of Medicine Bayamon, Puerto Rico Private MD school	I: $20000 O: $27000 for 2005	Degree: Yes MCAT: Yes	GPA: 3.31 MCAT: 20.1	
University at Buffalo State University of New York School of Medicine & Biomedical Sciences Buffalo, NY, USA Public MD school	I: $18800 O: $33500 for 2005	Degree: No MCAT: Yes	GPA: 3.54 MCAT: 28.5	
University of Alabama School of Medicine Birmingham, AL, USA Public MD school	I: $11365 O: $34095 for 2005	Degree: Yes MCAT: Yes		
University of Arizona College of Medicine Tucson, AZ, USA Public MD school	I: $14359 O: $0 for 2005	Degree: No MCAT: Yes	GPA: 3.63 MCAT:	
University of Arkansas for Medical Sciences College of Medicine Little Rock, AR, USA Public MD school	I: $14088 O: $28176 for 2005	Degree: No MCAT: Yes	GPA: 3.66 MCAT: 27	
University of California Los Angeles - Drew Los Angeles, CA, USA Private MD school		Degree: Yes MCAT: Yes		
University of California, Davis, School of Medicine Sacramento, CA, USA Public MD school	I: $0 O: $12245 for 2005	Degree: No MCAT: Yes	GPA: 3.55 MCAT: 31.8	

University of California, Irvine, College of Medicine Irvine, CA, USA Public MD school	I: $0 O: $12245 for 2005	Degree: No MCAT: Yes	GPA: 3.7 MCAT: 32
University of California, San Diego, School of Medicine La Jolla, CA, USA Public MD school	I: $0 O: $12245 for 2005	Degree: No MCAT: Yes	GPA: 3.8 MCAT: 32.1
University of California, San Francisco, School of Medicine San Francisco, CA, USA Public MD school	I: $0 O: $12245 for 2005	Degree: No MCAT: Yes	GPA: 3.76 MCAT: 33
University of Chicago Division of the Biological Sciences The Pritzker School of Medicine Chicago, IL, USA Private MD school	I: $32022 O: $32022 for 2005	Degree: No MCAT: Yes	GPA: 3.74 MCAT: 33.3
University of Cincinnati College of Medicine Cincinnati, OH, USA Public MD school	I: $22452 O: $39876 for 2005	Degree: No MCAT: Yes	GPA: 3.59 MCAT: 29.7
University of Colorado Health Sciences Center School of Medicine Denver, CO, USA Public MD school	I: $20718 O: $72291 for 2005	Degree: Yes MCAT: Yes	GPA: 3.7 MCAT: 31
University of Connecticut School of Medicine Farmington, CT, USA Public MD school	I: $15870 O: $36110 for 2005	Degree: No MCAT: Yes	GPA: 3.66 MCAT: 30.5
University of Florida College of Medicine Gainesville, FL, USA Public MD school	I: $18016 O: $46404 for 2005	Degree: Yes MCAT: Yes	GPA: 3.71 MCAT: 30.75
University of Hawaii John A. Burns School of Medicine Honolulu, HI, USA Public MD school	I: $16080 O: $29784 for 2005	Degree: No MCAT: Yes	GPA: 3.63 MCAT: 28
University of Illinois College of Medicine Chicago, IL, USA Public MD school	I: $24122 O: $52176 for 2005	Degree: Yes MCAT: Yes	GPA: 3.48 MCAT: 29.1
University of Iowa Roy J. and Lucille A. Carver College of Medicine Iowa City, IA, USA Public MD school	I: $19020 O: $38226 for 2005	Degree: Yes MCAT: Yes	GPA: 3.7 MCAT: 30
University of Kansas School of Medicine Kansas City, KS, USA Public MD school	I: $18919 O: $34674 for 2005	Degree: Yes MCAT: Yes	GPA: 3.6 MCAT: 27.3
University of Kentucky College of Medicine Lexington, KY, USA Public MD school	I: $18342 O: $37316 for 2005	Degree: Yes MCAT: Yes	GPA: 3.64 MCAT: 28.74
University of Louisville School of Medicine Louisville, KY, USA Public MD school	I: $18040 O: $40406 for 2005	Degree: No MCAT: Yes	GPA: 3.6 MCAT: 27.6
University of Maryland School of Medicine Baltimore, MD, USA Public MD school	I: $19277 O: $35144 for 2005	Degree: No MCAT: Yes	GPA: 3.63 MCAT: 30

University of Massachusetts Medical School Worcester, MA, USA Public MD school	I: $8352 O: $0 for 2005	Degree: Yes MCAT: Yes	GPA: 3.6 MCAT: 31.2
University of Medicine and Dentistry of New Jersey - School of Osteopathic Medicine (UMDNJ-SOM) Stratford, NJ, USA Public DO school	I: $20742 O: $32360 for 2004	Degree: Yes MCAT: Yes	GPA: MCAT: 26
University of Miami Leonard M. Miller School of Medicine Miami, FL, USA Private MD school	I: $29298 O: $38504 for 2005	Degree: No MCAT: Yes	GPA: 3.66 MCAT: 29.1
University of Michigan Medical School Ann Arbor, MI, USA Public MD school	I: $21578 O: $33930 for 2005	Degree: No MCAT: Yes	GPA: 3.7 MCAT: 33.3
University of Minnesota Medical School - Duluth Duluth, MN, USA Public MD school		Degree: Yes MCAT: Yes	GPA: 3.67 MCAT: 28
University of Minnesota Medical School - Twin Cities Minneapolis, MN, USA Public MD school	I: $26607 O: $33502 for 2005	Degree: Yes MCAT: Yes	GPA: 3.67 MCAT: 31.1
University of Mississippi School of Medicine Jackson, MS, USA Public MD school	I: $7649 O: $14327 for 2005	Degree: No MCAT: Yes	GPA: 3.66 MCAT: 28.2
University of Missouri-Columbia School of Medicine Columbia, MO, USA Public MD school	I: $20909 O: $41634 for 2005	Degree: Yes MCAT: Yes	GPA: 3.71 MCAT: 28.7
University of Missouri-Kansas City School of Medicine Kansas City, MO, USA Public MD school	I: $26817 O: $52060 for 2005	Degree: Yes MCAT: Yes	
University of Nebraska College of Medicine Omaha, NE, USA Public MD school	I: $19568 O: $45888 for 2005	Degree: No MCAT: Yes	GPA: 3.65 MCAT: 28.5
University of Nevada School of Medicine Reno, NV, USA Public MD school	I: $10588 O: $29398 for 2005	Degree: No MCAT: Yes	GPA: 3.6 MCAT: 27.1
University of New England College of Osteopathic Medicine (UNECOM) Biddeford, ME, USA Private DO school	I: $33545 O: $33545 for 2004	Degree: No MCAT: Yes	GPA: MCAT: 25.3
University of New Mexico School of Medicine Albuquerque, NM, USA Public MD school	I: $12893 O: $37032 for 2005	Degree: No MCAT: Yes	GPA: 3.51 MCAT: 28.2
University of North Carolina at Chapel Hill School of Medicine Chapel Hill, NC, USA Public MD school	I: $9335 O: $33001 for 2005	Degree: No MCAT: Yes	GPA: 3.65 MCAT: 31.3
University of North Dakota School of Medicine and Health Sciences Grand Forks, ND, USA	I: $18908 O: $50482 for 2005	Degree: No MCAT: Yes	GPA: 3.71 MCAT: 26

Public MD school

University of Oklahoma College of Medicine Oklahoma City, OK, USA Public MD school	I: $15140 O: $37228 for 2005	Degree: Yes MCAT: Yes	GPA: 3.68 MCAT: 27.81	
University of Pennsylvania School of Medicine Philadelphia, PA, USA Private MD school	I: $36976 O: $36976 for 2005	Degree: Yes MCAT: Yes	GPA: 3.78 MCAT: 34.2	
University of Pittsburgh School of Medicine Pittsburgh, PA, USA Private MD school	I: $32218 O: $36965 for 2005	Degree: Yes MCAT: Yes	GPA: 3.7 MCAT: 32.7	
University of Puerto Rico School of Medicine San Juan, Puerto Rico MD school	I: $6650 O: $13965 for 2005	Degree: No MCAT: Yes	GPA: 3.68 MCAT: 23	
University of Rochester School of Medicine and Dentistry Rochester, NY, USA Private MD school	I: $34450 O: $34450 for 2005	Degree: Yes MCAT: Yes	GPA: 3.67 MCAT: 30.7	
University of South Alabama College of Medicine Mobile, AL, USA Public MD school	I: $12254 O: $24508 for 2005	Degree: No MCAT: Yes	GPA: 3.7 MCAT: 29.1	
University of South Carolina School of Medicine Columbia, SC, USA Public MD school	I: $19520 O: $56446 for 2005	Degree: Yes MCAT: Yes	GPA: 3.54 MCAT: 27	
University of South Dakota School of Medicine Sioux Falls, SD, USA Public MD school	I: $13324 O: $31700 for 2005	Degree: Yes MCAT: Yes	GPA: 3.62 MCAT: 26.6	
University of South Florida College of Medicine Tampa, FL, USA Public MD school	I: $16449 O: $48533 for 2005	Degree: Yes MCAT: Yes	GPA: 3.7 MCAT: 28.6	
University of Tennessee Health Science Center College of Medicine Memphis, TN, USA Public MD school	I: $17522 O: $34406 for 2005	Degree: Yes MCAT: Yes	GPA: 3.61 MCAT: 28	
University of Texas Medical Branch at Galveston Galveston, TX, USA Public MD school	I: $8350 O: $21450 for 2005	Degree: Yes MCAT: Yes	GPA: 3.64 MCAT: 27	
University of Texas Medical School at Houston Houston, TX, USA Public MD school	I: $9775 O: $22875 for 2005	Degree: Yes MCAT: Yes	GPA: 3.64 MCAT: 28.4	
University of Texas Medical School at San Antonio San Antonio, TX, USA Public MD school	I: $9550 O: $23725 for 2005	Degree: No MCAT: Yes	GPA: 3.5 MCAT: 28	
University of Texas Southwestern Medical Center at Dallas Southwestern Medical School Dallas, TX, USA Public MD school	I: $9325 O: $22425 for 2005	Degree: Yes MCAT: Yes	GPA: 3.8 MCAT: 32.5	

University of Utah School of Medicine
  Salt Lake City, UT, USA
  Public MD school
I: $16973 Degree: Yes GPA: 3.6
O: $32133 MCAT: Yes MCAT: 30
for 2005

University of Vermont College of Medicine
  Burlington, VT, USA
  Public MD school
I: $2400   Degree: No   GPA: 3.5
O: $42010 MCAT: Yes MCAT: 28.35
for 2005

University of Virginia School of Medicine
  Charlottesville, VA, USA
  Public MD school
I: $27073 Degree: Yes GPA: 3.7
O: $37073 MCAT: Yes MCAT: 32.1
for 2005

University of Washington School of Medicine
  Seattle, WA, USA
  Public MD school
I: $13952 Degree: Yes GPA: 3.69
O: $33790 MCAT: Yes MCAT: 31.1
for 2005

University of Wisconsin Medical School
  Madison, WI, USA
  Public MD school
I: $21202 Degree: Yes GPA: 3.74
O: $32326 MCAT: Yes MCAT: 30.8
for 2005

Vanderbilt University School of Medicine
  Nashville, TN, USA
  Private MD school
I: $33200 Degree: Yes GPA: 3.77
O: $33200 MCAT: Yes MCAT: 32.38
for 2005

Virginia Commonwealth University School of Medicine
  Richmond, VA, USA
  Public MD school
I: $22385 Degree: No   GPA: 3.46
O: $36534 MCAT: Yes MCAT: 28.5
for 2005

Wake Forest University School of Medicine
  Winston-Salem, NC, USA
  Private MD school
I: $34006 Degree: No   GPA: 3.6
O: $34006 MCAT: Yes MCAT: 30
for 2005

Washington University in St. Louis School of Medicine
  St. Louis, MO, USA
  Private MD school
I: $39720 Degree: No   GPA: 3.82
O: $39720 MCAT: Yes MCAT: 36.4
for 2005

Wayne State University School of Medicine
  Detroit, MI, USA
  Public MD school
I: $21695 Degree: Yes GPA: 3.51
O: $45147 MCAT: Yes MCAT: 28
for 2005

West Virginia School of Osteopathic Medicine (WVSOM)
  Lewisburg, WV, USA
  Public DO school
I: $16618 Degree: No   GPA: 3.45
O: $40830 MCAT: Yes MCAT: 22.4
for 2004

West Virginia University School of Medicine
  Morgantown, WV, USA
  Public MD school
I: $14766 Degree: No   GPA: 3.69
O: $35764 MCAT: Yes MCAT: 27.1
for 2005

Western University of Health Sciences/College of Osteopathic
Medicine of the Pacific (Western U/COMP)
  Pomona, CA, USA
  Private DO school
I: $33270 Degree: No   GPA:
O: $33270 MCAT: Yes MCAT: 28
for 2004

Wright State University School of Medicine
  Dayton, OH, USA
  Public MD school
I: $20988 Degree: No   GPA: 36.5
O: $29712 MCAT: Yes MCAT: 29.8
for 2005

Yale University School of Medicine
  New Haven, CT, USA
  Private MD school
I: $37280 Degree: Yes GPA: 3.74
O: $37280 MCAT: Yes MCAT: 33.6
for 2005

Application Essays and Personal Statements

The personal statement accompanies your AMCAS and non-AMCAS applications to medical schools. You will also receive supplementary applications (secondaries) with specific long answer essays, and much of the advice we will go over below will also apply to your secondaries. Sometimes referred to as the "statement of purpose" or "personal essay," this is your opportunity to state who you are, where you are coming from and where you are going professionally. The statement is one of five or six central factors that go into making admission decisions--the others are GPA, test scores, letters of recommendation, experience and the interview. A poorly written statement can keep you out of the program of your choice, while a well-written statement may get you to the interview and prove to be a deciding factor in your acceptance. You want to garner the admissions committee's interest with your personal statement and secondary essays. Someone who reads your essay and does not know you should find you interesting and want to meet you.

What do Admissions Committee Members Look for in the Statement?

Admissions Committee members will be looking mainly at style and content. They read countless applications and essays in a fairly short time and as a result, many readers skim personal statements. Therefore, you should be concise (but not too brief) and use key words and action verbs throughout your statement. For this same reason, you should try to capture your reader's attention by describing any out-of-the-ordinary and interesting things you have done. If possible try to incorporate warmth and feeling in your essay. This is not an exercise in academic writing; it is ok to use the word "I". Instill some humanity in the statement, and give them a reason to want to interview you. Write it as if you were writing a newspaper article about yourself in the sense that you want to answer the "who, what, where, when, and how" of you and your journey toward medicine.

What Should You Do to Get Started?

Think about what kind of information you want the admissions committee to know about you that is not fully described elsewhere in the application. There may be some overlap with information in the application, but it will be presented in a different way.

Some questions that will help you get started:

- What is your first recollection about doctors and the medical field? What was your reaction to it?
- Who do you know who is a doctor? What do you like, respect, admire about that person?
- Why do you want to be a doctor, dentist, or veterinarian? Why not a nurse/ counselor? social worker/ researcher, Vet Technician, or Dental Assistant?
- Who is your role model and why? What have you learned from this person?
- What is the most memorable experience you had in your health related/social service experience?
- I'm the dean of a medical school, why should I let you in?
- What are two things about you that make you different from anyone else you know?
- When did you discover your interest in the field? Profession?
- Why are you interested in the field? Profession?
- What academic strengths do you possess? For example: above average grades, leadership roles in specific courses, teaching assistant/lab assistant experience.
- Are there some extraordinary circumstances that may need to be discussed? For example: your grades suffered in a particular semester/year because of a demanding work schedule, illness, or family problems. Before you venture down these roads please speak with us we may be able to address these issues more safely in our letter.

- What honors/awards have you received? For example: scholarships, awards bestowed by an organization of which you are a member, recognition for work in the community.
- What research activities have you participated in? For example: research assistant, slide prep, data entry/analysis, and survey development/administration.
- What extracurricular activities have you participated in? For example: membership/office in a campus organization, membership/office in a professional/community organization.
- What volunteer experience do you have?
- What relevant work experience do you have?
- What specific areas of interest do you have within the field of medicine?
- Why will you make a strong addition to this program? What strengths do you bring with you?
- What are your career goals once you complete your education?
- Have you had meaningful life experiences: careers, travel, Peace Corps., graduate degrees, etc., that would make you stand out from the rest. Discuss your non-traditional background, using it to highlight your journey to medicine.
- What activities and organizations have you been involved with on campus?
- Why do you enter these activities and organizations, and what do you feel you contribute to them? What do you get out of them?
- What sort of people-oriented activities are you involved in and why?
- What sort of summer activities are you involved in?
- What is the extent of exposure to medicine that you have?
- What leadership qualities do you possess and how have you demonstrated them?
- What do your peers think of you? How has this been demonstrated?
- What is the rigor of your academic schedule, as you see it?
- Are you performing up to your academic potential? If not, why?
- Why do you feel medicine is the career for you?
- Are there any other careers that interest you?
- What are some of your strengths and/or weaknesses?
- Can you evaluate your maturity, sensitivity, and compassion toward others?

- Have you ever been in trouble with the law or at school?

Make a list of all the information you want the admissions committee to have about you. Organize the items on your list into groups of ideas that seem to fit together naturally.

Spend some time on these, because you'll need to address them either through your Personal Statement, your list of Postsecondary Experiences, your interview, or some combination of the three.

Writing Your Statement

1. Read the question on the application before you write your answer. Many times applicants have their own agenda when writing and forget to focus on the question asked of them. After you are finished, reflect on the question and make sure your answer is exactly that--an answer.

2. Write when you write and edit when you edit! Your first draft should be straight from the heart, brutally honest, and inclusive of all the information you think will be useful to the admissions committee; you can edit later.

3. Do not just write what you think they want to read. It will seem too contrived. Speak from your heart; trying to convey an honest representation of who you are is the best policy. You can't fabricate a person that does not exist.

4. A personal statement should be a reflection of your personality. By reading your personal statement the admissions committee should be able to develop a better understanding of you. An effective essay lets the reader know you would be interesting person to interview.

5. Consider the readers of your application. Admissions committees are made up of persons who are proud to be associated with the profession, and are gatekeepers of the profession. Do not overly criticize medicine or physicians.

6. For Post-Bac Students: As a student, most of you have nontraditional backgrounds, which need to be explained. You can use your background to illustrate your maturity, new-found study skills, motivation, direction, and focus.

You have given up time, money, and other valuable things to make this change in your life and career direction. This says a great deal about you.

7. No whining and no excuses--do not write a laundry list of personal problems. The essay should be upbeat, illustrating how you have turned adversity to strength. An explanation is always better than an excuse. Owning up to your own contribution to academic problems is a better way to go than blaming someone else or not taking ownership of what you did to contribute to a problem. For example, if you have changed your study habits and are now successful, discuss how you changed or modified your approach.

8. Avoid the unusual. A personal statement in the form of a ceramic yucca or haiku is not a good idea.

9. Be specific and provide details. Your details and experiences are what make your personal statement unique and will impress the reader. Document your conclusions with examples.

10. Do not simply supply a list of accomplishments and experiences without addressing how those experiences helped you determine your career objective or helped you to better understand yourself and your role as a potential health care provider. A laundry list of accomplishments may appear egotistical. Everything in your personal statement should have a reason for being included. Formulate conclusions that reflect the meaningfulness of your experiences.

11. Be prepared to write several drafts. Start early. Waiting until the last minute is never a good idea. After you have written your statement, set it aside for a day or two (or more) then revisit it. When you read it again, you may be in a different frame of mind and will be fresh to revise.

12. Organize your ideas logically. Many personal statements are organized chronologically. Other statements are organized by topic (e.g. history, academic background, experience, and community service) or by theme or thesis (e.g. what will make a good physician in the year 2010 and how/why you would be that person). Whatever style you choose, it is imperative that you provide the reader with some reference points so that he does not have to spend time sorting out your information.

13. Set the proper tone for your statement. Remember that this is your chance for them to know you more personally and you should take full advantage of this opportunity. Avoid the use of clichés. Avoid the use of slang and/or sentences or phrases that give conversational or chatty tone to your essay. In general, avoid criticism so that you do not run the risk of offending your readers. You are writing for professionals, so be professional in your choice of words.

Some Pointers for Polishing Your Personal Statement

1. Vary your sentence structure from time to time to keep your reader interested. What works is variety, controlling the rhythm of passages through the mixing of short, long and intermediate sentences. Several short sentences after several longer ones, on the other hand, can be equally effective as a brisk conclusion.

2. Do not try to be clever or humorous unless you are absolutely certain you can pull it off with finesse. An application to a graduate or health profession school is serious business.

3. Use the active voice. Put the spotlight on you rather than on someone or something else.
   Weak: I was employed by the veterinary hospital to assist…
   Better: I assisted in examination of…

4. Watch for sentence fragments, run-on sentences, and dangling phrases or ideas.

5. Use action-packed, descriptive verbs and be careful not to switch tenses. Avoid ending sentences with a preposition (e.g. with, of).

6. Do not be unnecessarily wordy.
   Weak: After the course was finished, I was sure that I wanted to spend my entire life in daily contact with the world of medicine.
   Better: That course convinced me my future was in medicine. (Then you can go on to say how and in what way you were convinced.)

7. Make sure your statement is organized, and avoid redundancy. If it is too long or rambling, it will appear undisciplined and out of focus.

8. When using an acronym, give the entire name when it first appears followed by the acronym in parentheses.

9. Have several people review your draft--friends, family, faculty and staff. They may know some things about you that you omitted, and may be more objective and give you an honest opinion on how you are coming across.
10. This is an exercise in perfection. Poor grammar, spelling, punctuation, incomplete sentences are not acceptable under any circumstances and will weaken your application.

Through the essay, the admissions committee wants to see who you are. They only have your "sterile" application in front of them, listing all of your accomplishments, your coursework and other information. The personal statement allows them to see you as a person, not just in terms of numbers and lists of accomplishments. The statement is also used by the people who interview you. They usually review your file and essay before the interview.

Other People's Statements

Reading other people's statements will most likely make you feel inferior since you have not even started to think of yours. You will be astonished about how well other people are able to write, how neat their stories are, how entertaining their essay is and how well it flows.

What you don't see is that they went through the same turmoil you are going through now, that they may have spent several months writing, rewriting and refining every sentence and every word to make it flow and sound that good. They may even have involved an English professor or other people to help them finalize their statements.

So, don't panic or think you could never come up with something that good. By the time you're done, people will be in awe about your statement when they first start out writing theirs.

Reading other applicant's essays may lead to problems - you may end up using their language and expressions rather than your own.

The school is really interested in hearing about you and your motivations in becoming a physician. The trick in telling them about yourself is telling stories or writing about what you have done to show how you interact, what type of person you are - and what feelings and motivations you have.

So, rather than saying, "I am compassionate, hard-working, love to help people and have all the qualities to become a great physician...", which may all be correct, factual statements about you, you need to spend some time showing this through activities you have done.

In short, they want to hear about you and your story as well as your motivations for medicine. Write about your feelings and motivations. What are the things that convinced you to pursue medicine? If you have dreamed of becoming a physician all your life, write about that. But you better have some evidence to support that claim in the form of stories, feelings, experiences that have validated that choice. Maybe you have had some serious event in your life that caused you to pursue medicine. Write about it.

Your statement does not have to be completely about pre-medical pursuits, etc. If you love sports or any other activity that totally defines you and has taught you great lessons or shows your positive qualities and attributes, you can use that as your story. The personal statement is intended to tell your story, whatever that story is. Just make sure that what you write about still meets the general idea and you answer the question "Why medicine?" and show how these qualities will make you a great physician.

You can capitalize on your unique situation. Are you a non-traditional student? Write about it. Write about why you changed your mind, what lead you to medicine.

How to come up with your Qualities

So, you think you are plain boring and have nothing to share?

Ask yourself and others (others often know you better than you do) about your qualities and make a list of them. Are you energetic, driven, focused, organized, a leader, a team player, compassionate. Come up with a list and pick the top 3 to 5 of them that really define you the most. Try to bring these qualities out as you write the statement. When your statement is done, ask yourself "Are each one of these reflected in this statement?" If not, try to rewrite some parts to incorporate them.

How to come up with your motivation for medicine

What made you decide to pursue medicine?
What events (shadowing, volunteering, or other events) appealed to you or "opened your eyes" or lead you down this path to medicine?
Imagine you had to convince your spouse or a close friend who is skeptical about your decision that medicine was your thing, what would you tell him or her? How would you back up your claim?
Do you love the sciences, the cutting edge of biology, curing diseases, dealing with people, helping others, intellectual stimulation, challenges?

If you are having a hard time with this, you probably haven't spend enough time with extra-curricular activities that involve you in patient care - whether actively or as an observer.

Don't overdo it

You want to sell yourself, but without bragging or giving the impression you are the best thing that ever happened. People reading your statements can immediately sense if you are insincere or bluffing. They have read thousands of statements throughout the years and are pros - so take them seriously. Don't lie, don't exaggerate too much, and don't brag. But stress your strong points.

Time Line & Procedures for Medical School Applications

STUDENTS APPLYING FOR ENTRANCE TO MEDICAL SCHOOL

November

- Thanksgiving Break
- Receive pre-registration packets and set up a meeting with your advisor to determine which classes you will be taking. Make sure you are on track in completing your premedical requirements.
- Meetings to discuss application process, time line, and letters of evaluation.

December

- Pre-registration
- Meetings to discuss application process, time line, and letters of evaluation.
- Begin winter break
- Begin studying for the MCAT. Possibly arrange to take an MCAT preparation course if you are taking the Spring MCAT
- Begin drafts of your personal statements
- Write or update your resume
- Fill out autobiographical form
- Make sure your credit rating and that of your parents are in good condition. These ratings may affect your loan applications for medical school.
- Have passport photograph taken and copied.
- Begin asking for letters of evaluation for Medical School

January

- Finish requesting letters of evaluation from faculty.

February

- updated resume
- autobiographical information form
- draft personal statement
- unofficial transcript
- individual faculty waivers to each professor as required
- If you have done this already, register if you are taking the Spring MCAT.

March

- updated resume
- autobiographical information form
- draft personal and goal statements
- list of faculty/staff evaluators
- unofficial transcript (available from the portal)
- Letter Packet Waiver Form

May

- Fill out web based version of the AMCAS or ACOMAS available online

AAMC	MD (Allopathic)	http://www.aamc.org/students/amcas/start.htm
ACOMAS	DO (Osteopathic)	http://aacomas.aacom.org
TMDSAS	Some MD, DO & Dental Programs in Texas	http://www.utsystem.edu/tmdsas
OMSAS	Allopathic Medical Schools in Ontario Canada	http://www.ouac.on.ca/omsas

- Send away for non-AMCAS, non-ADSAS, non-VMCAS applications.
- Continue to study for the MCAT if you have not taken it.

- Have all your transcripts sent to AMCAS, ACOMAS, and TMDSAS and/or non-AMCAS schools from all U.S. colleges and universities you have attended.
- Check that all letters of evaluation have been received.

Interpret MCAT scores and GPA with premedical advisor

Make first draft of AMCAS essay.

Send for medical school catalogs.

June

- Register for the August MCAT (if appropriate).
- June 1 to June 30, 2006: Send in AMCAS and ACOMAS applications even if you are completing your premedical courses over the summer or plan to take the August MCAT.
- Submit non-AMCAS applications.
- Reminder—Make sure you have had all transcripts from all colleges and universities sent to AMCAS/ACOMAS/VMCAS/ADSAS/and Non AMCAS Schools.
- By the third week you should have received Spring MCAT scores.
- Revise and polish AMCAS essay

August

- Fill out your secondary applications and return them as soon as you get them.
- Inform premedical committee where to send your composed recommendation letter (if your school has such a committee).
- Register for fall MCAT if scores were low and you feel you are now better prepared.
- Take the August MCAT if needed

September

- Continue to fill out secondary applications and get them in as soon as possible.
- Make sure that your applications are complete and that letters of recommendation have been received. Call to confirm if necessary.

October

- By the third week you should receive your Fall MCAT scores
- Make sure that all your application materials are completed for all the schools to which you have applied.
- By October 1 Early Decision (ED) candidates notified of Acceptance status.
- October 15 Initial deadline for some schools to submit AAMCAS Application

November:

- Be patient. Interviews will come.

December

- If you have taken additional coursework, have your transcripts forwarded to all the schools to which you have applied.

January

- Complete or renew your Federal Financial Aid Application (FAFSA). You can also take do this electronically at http://www.fafsa.ed.gov.
- Fill out GAPSFAS form for financial aid.
- Send updated transcripts if requested by schools

February:

If no one loves you by Valentine's Day, speak immediately with your premedical advisor. He or he may be able to call on your behalf.

March

- All medical schools should have made enough acceptances to fill their entering class.
- If you are wait-listed, send a letter expressing continued interest.

May

- Medical School Applicants: by the 15th, all candidates who have acceptances are required to select the school of their choice. **You can be involuntarily withdrawn from all schools for holding multiple acceptances after this deadline.**

April August:

- Acceptance letters are still sent out, so stay calm. Made sure medical schools can reach you or a family member by telephone at all time.

Recommendation Letters

Overview

Recommendation letters are one of the criteria admission committees use in the admissions process and are, therefore, one important part of your application. To get good letters, participation in extra-curricular activities and positive interactions with faculty are important since both provide you with great recommendation letters written on your behalf.

Admissions Committees see on the application what activities you have listed, but recommendation letters tell them about how you interact with people in activities, and stress your good qualities.

I put a lot of weight on recommendations when I look at someone's record. I pay particular attention to what people say about the applicant's personal qualities. That is why you should choose with care the people you ask to recommend you. I prefer to see a letter from an assistant professor who led a seminar you were involved in, than a nationally recognized full professor who had you in lecture and says that you got an A in his/her course but doesn't know you very well. Try to get letters from anyone you can that knows you well and in an objective fashion. Someone like a research advisor, your supervisor at work, your academic advisor, a faculty person in residence. These people are more likely to know you well and have more to say about you. A local physician you did some volunteer work with is also a good choice, but not somebody who is a friend of your family

and only knows you in that capacity. It is also very useful to have a
committee letter from your school where they pool all your letters and
write a composite highlighting the high points. These save the
admissions committee people a lot of time. Make yourself known when
working with professors on class projects, and ask to do some
independent work. These things will set you apart from the pack. Also,
when you ask for a letter, and ask for the letter as early as
possible, give the person a way out - ask them if they can write you a
strong letter (not just an average one). Make it easy for them to
write the letter by giving them a deadline and including some info
about yourself together with a pre-addressed, self-stamped envelope.

Letters of recommendation are essential to your application to medical school. The
people who review your application rely heavily on the opinions of professors and
supervisors who have direct experience with your work. Therefore, it is very important
that you plan early and make contacts throughout your undergraduate career with people
who will be able to write detailed and enthusiastic letters for you.

You should ask for letters from professors, employers, supervisors, or other people in
positions of authority who will be able to say something substantial about you, that is,
something more than that they know your name or that you passed their class.

Ask people who have a sense of your personality and have high opinion of you.
Sometimes you may have to make a concerted effort to make an impression, especially if
your potential letter writer is a busy person or if you are one student in a class of 200.
That is why it is essential to plan early and cultivate relationships with people who will
be able to attest to your character later. If you have contact with someone who could be a
reference, make sure he or she gets to know who you are and what you are doing, and
above all, do it well.

Medical schools are very interested in finding out about your oral skills, research abilities
and writing skills. Letters can focus on any one or all of these topics. Or you may choose

to seek letters of recommendation from people who have knowledge of your performance in any of these areas.

Ask someone to write a letter while you are fresh in their mind, even if you do not need the letter immediately. Professors and employers with whom you have little day to day contact will forget quickly the qualities which made you notable earlier. If you are asking a professor, ask him or her as soon as the class is over. Ask employers when you are leaving a position or when you have completed a project. You will probably want to provide a resume, an exceptional paper your wrote for this professor, or a personal data sheet about your work in the class to refresh the professor's memory. He or she will greatly appreciate it when sitting down to write your letter.

Most people who think well of you will be happy to write a letter of recommendation if you simply tell them the purpose of the letter and the deadline by which you need it. Be specific about the purpose of letter so your reference can tailor his or her comments to your needs.

If you are not sure of your reference's opinion of your work, ask whether he or she is able to write a strong letter for you to make sure they are willing to write something substantial and positive. If not, ask someone else. The last thing you need is a superficial or luke-warm letter which could make someone reviewing your application think twice.

Bad Letters

Letters that merely state you were present are worthless. A doctor's opinion that you would be a great physician without any stated supporting evidence is also worthless. Letters that don't stress your personal strengths and qualities are worthless.

And you really don't want worthless letters. You need great letters.

Great Letters

What will help you are descriptions that show what type of person you are so that the admissions office can see who you are and what you are like. In a great letter you should be able to find strong positive descriptions of your personal characteristics and your attitude towards medicine that will make you a great physician. You should see statements that explain to the admissions people why you would be a great addition to the medical community.

The letter writer has to support the recommendation he or she is making on your behalf with evidence, writing about your qualities rather than just stating that you will be a fine physician or that you spent so and so many hours shadowing.

Best letters are from people you have spent some time with so they could get to know you. That's why it is important to shadow physicians for more than just a few hours.

Faculty Letters

For faculty letters, make sure that the faculty member gets to know you by name. If he/she cannot greet you by name in the hallway, you should find someone else to write a letter for you or do everything you can to get to know him/her.

Here are some more specific suggestions.
In Physics and Organic Chemistry, homework or assignments can be intense. You may only have to turn in very little or none of your homework or assigned problems for grading but may have plenty of assigned material to work through on your own. When one of the problems doesn't make sense, this presents an opportunity to ask your professor something, use them as an excuse to interact with your professor instead of just bypassing them. You need excuses to get to know your professor for a good letter, so use them. Go to your professor and ask him/her about the problem.

In your biology course, if you are learning about a topic, find some extra info in your text, maybe something that was not directly assigned reading, or something that is difficult to understand (maybe you understand it, but you can ask for some clarification). You can ask about something that is related or still to be covered, but hasn't been covered yet in lecture.

What you will gain from this:
1. The faculty member will get to know you if you do this several times during the semester.
2. It indicates you are interested in the material enough to ask.
3. It shows you work hard, esp. since you are doing extra work besides the minimum required to turn in.
4. It gives you opportunity to mention you are going to med school and other topics to build a relationship.

If you don't talk to your professor, you will only be an unknown student in the class and the result is a very impersonal letter, which is worthless. Focus on a couple of faculty members (preferably in the sciences, but any will do) to do this with. Pick someone you can connect with or who just someone who seems nice and easy going.

The reality is that most people don't hang out with their professors, and some but not all professors will tend not to remember you if you took a class with them 2 years ago. If you did well in their class, go to them anyway and be prepared. Tell them you're applying to medical school, give them your resume or CV (list all honors, interests, etc), your transcript and a letter outlining why you want to go to medical school, why you're a good candidate--so that they know your interests. Provide them with as much good, positive information as you can.

If you took a class and wrote a paper that the professor liked, there is a good chance he or she will remember you and will be willing to write a good letter. Seminar classes that are small and allow for much interaction and class participation are rare in the sciences but more common in the non-sciences and are also good opportunities to show to professors that you care and are a good, intellectually capable student--which translates into a good recommendation.

In fact if you're a freshman, sophomore or junior and thinking about applying to medical school, it is never to early to ask for recommendations. Always sign to waive your rights to read your recommendation. BE WARY. A bad letter is worse than no letter.

How to ask for a recommendation letter

Physicians
Once you get to the end of your shadowing time, ask the physician: "Would you be able to write me a positive letter of recommendation for my med school application?" or "Do you have any reservations writing a positive letter of recommendation for me?"

Make sure you ask for a positive letter. Also, be sure to ask if he can honestly give you a good letter. If he cannot, thank him and ask someone else. Most letter writers are not cruel enough to say they would write you a positive letter and then write a bad one. Usually, if you ask, they will be honest and tell you that they can give you a great recommendation or tell you that they will not be able to, for whatever reason (it does happen).

Faculty
Same story. Ask for a positive letter and get their guarantee that they can write a great one. If not, don't have them write it. You need a great letter, nothing less.

If they have any hesitation or concerns about writing a great letter, thank them and ask someone else.

You have to be firm on this. Don't be shy. Make sure you ask. They will usually be up-front and tell you if they cannot give you a stellar letter. You want the best and you can only be assured of that by asking for one bluntly.

What a letter writer may want from you

Often, the letter writer may request a resume or curriculum vitae, listing your major accomplishments, schooling, etc. You may be asked to provide some additional biographical information about yourself or why you are interested in medicine. So, be prepared to provide this information if necessary. You may even consider providing this information without being asked for it to allow the letter writer to personalize the letter even more. Most likely, you will be asked for this information, anyway, so be ready for it.

What to do with letters

Most pre-med advising offices (or student affairs offices) at colleges and universities will give you a choice between having an open or a closed student file in which they collect all documents pertinent to your medical school application, including recommendation letters written on your behalf. You usually have to sign a statement and decide at the beginning, when your file is first created, if you want your file to be open or closed. If you ask medical schools which type of file is best to choose, some will tell you that they don't care. Don't believe them. Some medical schools will only consider recommendation letters that were kept in a closed file and by far all schools prefer closed files to open files. So, what's the difference?

Open or closed files

Open file: You, as the student, have full access to all documents placed in your file. After a recommendation letter (or any other document) is received, you have full access to it and can look at anything in your file at any time. Most faculty members and others writing recommendation letters for you want to know in advance if your file is open or closed. If it is open, they are less likely to write negatively about you. When it is closed they have nothing to fear and write frankly. Therefore, medical schools prefer (and some outright require) that you have a closed file to ensure a more unbiased appraisal. That's why it is so important to ask letter writers frankly if they are able to write a very good letter without reservations up-front. You won't be able to see it once it is in your file.

Faculty members usually know the drill and you'll not see the letter they write for you. With physicians, many don't know about your file and they may either send their letter directly to the pre-med office or hand you a sealed envelope to deliver yourself. I'd recommend asking them for a second copy of the letter for your own records. Some pre-med offices require the physician to mail a letter directly to them or notify the physician that your file is closed. If the physician, therefore, does not provide a copy for you, I would still recommend asking for a personal copy for your own records a few weeks or months later, letting the physician know you'd appreciate a copy if possible, but that he/she is not required to give you one. Or, if the physician would prefer to keep the letter confident without showing it to you, you'd understand and have no problem with that. Most physicians should not have a problem with your request.

Who should write letters for you

Physicians you spent time with

Managers of places you volunteered/worked at in clinical settings

Faculty who taught you

Faculty/mentors you did research with

No personal friends, family, colleagues, or others should write letters for you.

Getting your personal copy of the letters

You should be able to get a personal copy from everyone with the exception of faculty, maybe, since they may be hesitant and most likely familiar with the closed file. If you have more letters than medical schools require, you can then choose the best ones to send to them. Most medical schools specify what types of letters and how many they want (usually 1-4) when you get your secondary application materials from the medical school.

Most medical schools only want one physician letter sent to them. If you have a letter from several physicians you can decide which is better and instruct your pre-med office to send that letter only. Similarly, if you have four or five faculty letters and the medical school only requires two, you can choose which two to have the office send. If you really don't know which to choose, go by your gut feeling. Some pre-med offices may not let students choose which letters to send, anyway.

Letter timing

Recommendation letters are sent directly to medical schools from either your undergrad pre-med office or from the letter writers. You will have to tell your pre-med office or committee (or the letter writer) which letters to send from your file and which schools to send them to. Typically, when you receive your secondary application materials from the medical school, they provide you with information about what kind of letters they want from you (e.g. two faculty and one physician letter or one pre-med committee letter, one physician letter and one faculty letter, or whatever) and where to send them.

Letter types

Most medical schools require a pre-med committee letter to be sent and an additional 1 to 3 other letters written by faculty or physicians in your behalf. Only submit what they ask for. If you have more letters or different letters than what they want, don't send the additional letters - they just clutter your file and your best letters may not get read at all. It is recommended that you don't send any school more than 3 or 4 letters total.

A Pre-Medical Committee writes what is called a "committee letter." Basically, you need to ask at least one professor from one of the non-Biology sciences to write a letter for you, and at least two others from the non-science disciplines. I would do this either over the summer when you're filling out the AMCAS or very early on in the semester. This allows the professor time to work on it and write you a great letter. If you've done an internship or had a medically related job, definitely get a letter from your supervisor.

Most schools don't want to get the letters until they get your secondary application, so make sure the letter is ready to send off when you need it. Also, the professors you ask to write the letters may occasionally forget about it for a little bit. Don't be afraid to *gently* remind them of the due date for the letter. A little friendly email never hurt anyone.

Usually the premedical committee at your school will ask you to provide them with three-to-four recommendations from faculty, or anyone else such as supervisor where you volunteered, done research, etc, etc. Two recommendations should be from science professors but not necessarily from those who taught your pre-med classes.

Pre-med Advisor and Committee

Pre-med Advisor

A competent pre-med advisor can make a big difference in guiding you through the admissions process successfully. Most students don't know anything about the admissions process or what to do to get into med school. The pre-med advisor is the first stop to help you determine what courses you may have to take at your university or college to graduate with a useful degree while also fulfilling all medical school course requirements at the same time.

Basically the advisor is there to help you gain admission to med school. The advisor will also be familiar with local shadowing, volunteer or clinical opportunities and may suggest faculty members who have previously worked well with pre-med undergraduate students on research. A pre-med advisor is also able to look at your unique situation and give you some direction and advice tailored to your unique circumstances.

Advisors typically have all kinds of useful information such as which med schools give tuition breaks or scholarships to students from your state, which med schools have admitted large numbers of students from your undergraduate institution or from your state in the past. These schools should be on the top of your list of medical schools to apply to.

Often, pre-med advisors or pre-med offices maintain email lists and distribute lots of good information, reminders about deadlines coming up and meetings or forums that you can attend. At these meetings you have a chance to meet staff from medical school admissions offices, local physicians and current medical students who share a wealth of knowledge about medical school admission and their own experiences.

In short, pre-med advisors are great resources. Go see your advisor. Hopefully your school has one. If not, check to see if another school in your area has one you can go make an appointment with.

Pre-med Committee

Many undergraduate institutions have pre-med committees, usually chaired by a pre-med advisor. Most medical schools require a letter of recommendation from a pre-med committee, or at least prefer a letter from a pre-med committee over other faculty letters. The pre-med committee may meet with you in an interview or other format to get to know you better. They then write a letter of recommendation in your behalf which is sent to the medical schools you have applied to about the same time you are returning your secondary applications.

Interviews

After you submit your AMCAS application, virtually all schools to which you're applying will send you a secondary application, which in some cases means no more than a request for another check anywhere from $50 to $100 or a check plus "short-essay" type answers to their questions.

The next stage of the process basically involves a lot of waiting, compulsively checking your mail 2-3 times a day in hope of finding a letter from medical schools. Often it takes a few months from the time you send in your secondary application for schools to acknowledge that they received your secondary application. This is very normal. It is helpful to write checks instead of money orders to each school--that way you know when they processed your application from the date that they redeemed your check. I would advise not to bother them with phone calls--you never know, it might work against you. But if you haven't heard from them for two months or otherwise before the New Year, call to inquire whether your application is complete--that is whether they have all recommendation letters, your application, etc. Unless your application is complete, they do not look at it.

Though some activity occurs before the New Year, especially if you apply really early (which is a very good idea), most of you will hear from schools after the New Year. Unless you're a super-candidate, eighty percent of letters you will get will be rejection letters, the rest will either inform you that you're invited for an interview or that your file has been put off for further review later on. Some schools will not send you any letter at all, which might mean they are still reviewing your file, or that they put it off for additional consideration. Alternatively it may just mean that they never got around to your application (esp. if you applied late in the process) or are too lazy (or too busy) to send you a rejection letter.

Invitation for an interview is the best news you can get at this point. Medical school admissions interview is what more than anything else separates premeds from preMD's. This is your time to shine, but hopefully if you get more than one interview. It is also an opportunity to shop around for the best deal in medical education. Believe it or not, you're not the only one who is trying to impress someone at this interview. Though you're not admitted yet, you will notice that medical schools themselves are trying to impress you. Once medical schools invite your for an interview they consider that you're the right material for medical school and that they are in competition for you with other schools.

Being invited for an interview is a good sign because it means you have made it past the initial applicant screenings. The interview is the admission committee's chance to observe how you interact and decide whether you would fit well in their program. They will also use the interview as an opportunity to assess your communication skills, critical thinking abilities, and motivation for the study and practice of medicine. It is also your chance to evaluate the program they offer to determine how well it suits your needs. For these reasons, the interview is an important opportunity for you to make a good impression.

Med schools only interview people that they are seriously considering, and most often times will not interview more than 10% of the total applicant pool. Considering the number of applicants, getting an interview is a great accomplishment.

So here's the bad news: an interview is only the halfway point in the journey. They have determined that your objective qualifications are good enough, and through letters of recommendation and your essay that you seem to have a good personality. Now it is all up to you to wow them with your stunning self and convince them that you would be an asset to their school.

The interview is an important factor in the medical school application process. The invitation to interview generally means that you are academically qualified for admission; however, schools cannot admit all those who are qualified. The school wants to take a closer look as you and determine if you have the personal qualities they consider important. Qualities such as enthusiasm, integrity, leadership ability, decision-making skills, honesty, and empathy are important in a health professional.

The interview provides the school with the chance to evaluate you. It also provides you with a chance to learn about the school. Your interview should be a conversation in which you both answer and ask questions, as opposed to a firing line where you wait for the interviewer's next question.

So what is it?

Basically, an interview is the school's chance to get to know the real you, and for you to evaluate the school and see how good a match it is with you. Almost all schools require you to go to their campus, unless it would pose an extreme difficulty to get there. Expect to be there all day. The interview itself will most likely be with a faculty member on the admissions board, although at some schools, a medical student can interview you. The interview will likely go for about 30 minutes to an hour. The rest of the day is filled with a tour and overviews of different aspects of the school.

Be prepared, but don't make a mountain out of a molehill. Most interviews are laid back, friendly encounters--no one is out there has the goal of pinning you down. Don't be afraid to say "I'm not sure," "I haven't thought about it" but these phrases should not be your answer to every question. No one I personally know has had a bad interview. Someone somewhere asked tough questions--sometimes the interviewer would even argue with you a bit but do not take it personally. The views you hold are your views, and unless you're a psycho and say something really outrageous that's fine, your interviewers do not expect you to agree with them. In fact, they might challenge your answer just to see if you can take criticism--and answer it or learn from it. Do not go on the defensive just for the sake of agreeing with your interviewer, if you think you're right. If you think he or she has a point, you can partially agree.

Basically, once you're invited for an interview you have been positively selected, to use a term from evolution, as a good candidate for medical school. My impression is that the role of the interview is to weed out weirdo's and also to select the most impressive candidates among acceptable candidates.

Your goal is to sell yourself. Be prepared to make a good sales pitch. Write down every positive characteristic you have and try to relate how it would make you an outstanding physician. Talk about your goals and achievements--this is the time to boast about your most miniscule achievements but do not exaggerate and don't be condescending! Be prepared for questions about your experiences. Tell stories--our civilization has been built by good storytellers. Rehearse your stories so that they sound good to the ear.

Some people feel just fine interacting with strangers. If you are this type of person, feel good about that, because you are starting with an advantage when it comes to the interview. If you feel like a fish out of water in social situations, you will need to work harder to prepare for your interview because, just as you will find throughout your life, first impressions count for a lot. Medical schools want to see someone with substance who can make the person sitting across from them feel comfortable. If you think about it, this is a pretty necessary feature of any doctor. Should you reach your goal of becoming a physician, you will probably be interacting with several dozen patients on any given day, and they will only become regular patients if they are at ease around you. A reputation as someone unpleasant to be around will severely limit business. It seems fair to expect social skills out of someone aspiring to such a social profession.

Think about your agenda for the interview and be prepared to guide the interview into subjects that present you in the best possible light.
Read and ask questions about the school you are going to be interviewing in. Come prepared with a copy of your resume just in case. Dress your best and conservatively, although women can wear something besides navy (everybody wears navy, if you wear something a different color people might remember you better). Make sure you talk to as many students as you can and ask them what they think of the place. Med school is hard work and people will be tired, but some places treat their students better than others and

you need to find this out. Try to stay for more than a day and explore the surroundings, if you can stay with one of the current students (many schools have volunteers for this, so ask when you get invited to the interview). Try to get as much information about the school as they get out of you.

Relax, breathe, and try not to pass out. The most important thing you can do is to be yourself. Remember, these people have interviewed thousands of people over the years. They can spot a snow job from a mile away. It's your personality that is going to get you into school. Trust your instincts and rely on yourself.

A few helpful hints. Show up early. You never want to keep your interviewer waiting. Treat all you meet, from the janitor to the chief of staff, as if they were the person interviewing you. During the interview, maintain strong eye contact with the interviewer, but don't stare him down, and try not to fidget too much. If you need a few seconds to compose your answer, take them. The interviewer won't mind waiting a few seconds to get a well thought out answer. Make sure you stay for the entire program that the admissions department has put together. Talk to the students who are there. There will always be student tour guides, and others there just to answer questions. They are the ones with the inside perspective. Ask them anything you want to know about the school, from the social life, to apartment hunting, to how much time they spend in class. They will know better than the faculty. After the interview, send a thank you card to your interviewer. It's a nice gesture and also lets them know that you are still interested in the school.

You may be interviewed alone by a single admissions person, alone by a group of admissions people, or with other applicants by a panel of admissions people. In some cases, the interviewer will have access to and knowledge of your academic and personal accomplishments. In other cases, the interviewer will have no knowledge of these things. Regardless of the circumstances, the following tips may help make your interview experience as pleasant and productive as it can be.

First, be prepared. Imagine what kinds of questions you would ask an applicant and be ready to answer them. Also, have a few questions of your own about the program or school. Be ready to explain why you are interested in this medical school and what draws you to the field of medicine. Practice interviewing with a friend, or schedule a pre-med interview with a Health Professions Advisor. You do not need to prepare by creating canned responses or producing a script. Rather, you should form a framework for your ideas, interests, and experiences from which to respond. You should also be prepared for the unexpected question and have the candor to say "I'm not sure of that," or "I haven't really thought through that issue."

Try to relax and be confident but not arrogant. Try to keep the interview conversational, but don't get rattled if you feel like you are being grilled. Just answer questions honestly and be yourself (as long as you are someone who is responsible, professional and sincere). Interviewers will be listening for responses which reflect both insight into the profession and the requisite motivation to achieve educational and professional objectives.

Continued nervousness is a bad thing in an interview situation.

You should be prepared to discuss yourself, the medical school, and general issues about health care. Make an honest assessment of yourself—identify your strengths and weaknesses. Review your application, secondary application, and transcripts before each interview. Make sure you are familiar with everything a potential interviewer may know about you.

The safest attire for an interview is a business suit. Blue is safe, but many people wear blue. If you look good in gray, brown, black, or tan this may be a better option—you will be appropriately dressed and not blend in to the others. Also, a fresh groomed appearance cannot help but make a good impression. This is not a time to make a statement, and avoid clothing or accessories, which may be distracting.

When meeting your interviewer, use a firm handshake; choose a seat which allows you good eye contact with the interviewer.

Be aware of any mannerisms or other personal habits that might detract from the interview. Do not twist in your chair, move your hands excessively while you talk, and fiddle with your clothing, hair or jewelry.

During the interview it is important to keep eye contact. Try not to mimic the facial expressions of interviewers—they may be very inexpressive on purpose to see how you react. Try not to look down.

Try to be comfortable and confident without appearing cocky or insincere. Smile and maintain a pleasant, interested manner.

Make sure you listen to each question carefully, and always provide specifics when giving your answers. Giving concrete answers that involve your academic and volunteer experiences give your answers tremendous credibility.

Remember to be yourself. Most interviewers want to get to know you. You are your own best advocate.

Be honest and do not embellish your history. Candor is essential. Any suspicion about your credibility or integrity can doom your acceptance.

Anticipate questions regarding any academic problems, and when you answer their questions do not be defensive or blame others for your shortcomings.

Do your homework about the schools. Go to their web sites and read about their histories, their rotation sites (hospitals/clinics), curriculum, and philosophy or mission statement. Formulate questions about the school which reflect your interest.

Expect questions about issues in modern society and medicine. When answering, organize your thoughts, state your opinions clearly, and be prepared to substantiate your opinions.

If you are treated inappropriately or asked illegal questions (e.g. personal, racist, and/or sexist) you should generally inform the admissions office/director you have interviewed with on the day it occurs so they can possibly make arrangements for you to have another interview. Many admissions directors will ask you to inform them the day of the interview if an interviewer asks any illegal questions such as are you married, do you have or are you planning to have children, etc… This happens very rarely.

Make your flight and hotel reservations early for best prices and availability. Before you book, ask the med school for hotels close by. Most of them have arrangements to give you a huge (sometimes 60% off) discount if you are flying in for an interview at the school. Also arrange transportation services (taxi or shuttle) the night before (ask the school or hotel).

Finally, send a thank-you note to your interviewers. Keep it short, but highlight aspects of the program that particularly interested you. After that, relax and watch your mail.

Timing

Schools typically contact you by mail or email to invite you to an interview. Most likely, they will offer you several days to choose from, sometimes spread out over several months. If at all possible, try to take the first interview day offered to you. Get right back with the school to schedule your interview so that your interview slot is reserved right away.

Interviewing on the first day possible is advantageous to you since the school has not yet filled most of the spots available in the class. Also, the earlier you attend the interview, the earlier you will be able to receive an offer.

Types of Interviews

There are several types of interviews which can be conducted as open, semi-open, or closed file interviews. Medical schools can have anywhere from 1-3 interviews for each applicant on the day they are interviewed. Interviewers can have formal lists of questions for the interviews, a general guideline of topics, or complete freedom to structure the interview.

Individual Interview — This is an interview that takes place with one interviewer. The interviewer can be an administrator, clinical faculty, basic science faculty, current MD student or MD/PhD student, alumni member, and/or retired faculty. Never underestimate the importance of the student interviews.

Group Interview — involves many candidates and either one or several interviewers. In most cases, this scenario is used to determine how candidates interact with other members of a group. (i.e., do you listen? interrupt? clarify? dominate? never say anything?)

Board/Panel Interview — is one candidate with more than one interviewer. You need to make sure you establish eye contact with all members of the panel.

Open Interview — the interviewers have all your application materials.

Semi-Open Interviews — the interviewers have only some basic information. Either they have all the non-cognitive information (personal statement, experiences, letters of evaluation) or all the cognitive (GPA, MCAT Scores, Transcripts).

Closed Interview — They have nothing about you except your name and maybe where you went to school.

Who gets interviews?

All medical schools are extremely selective in terms of who gets an interview. Generally, 5-10% of the applicant pool gets an interview.

What kind of questions do they ask at interviews?

Interviews are either open (the interviewer has seen your application/personal statement) or closed (the interviewer has not seen any of your application materials). The type of interview will greatly influence the types of questions asked (you will not know beforehand which type of interview you will get, so be prepared for both). Typical questions in an open interview are: (a) So tell me more about this-or-that on your application, (b) I noticed you volunteered for such-and-such, how did your experiences influence your decision to apply to medical school, (c) Tell me more about your family/your relationship with them, (d) Why did you pick your college as an undergraduate school? Most people consider closed interviews to be more difficult because the questions are less personal and broader. Typical closed interview questions are: (a) I haven't seen your file, so tell me about yourself, (b) What do you think of the Patients' Bill of Rights (or some other national legislation), (c) What do you think about fee-for-service medicine/HMOs/PPOs (or some other type of medical practice). Most interviews are a bit of both types, so be prepared for all sorts of topics. In my experience, the infamous question "Why do you want to be a doctor" is present in almost all interviews; be prepared to answer this question in a succinct and well-thought manner (i.e., responding "because I want to heal people" will certainly not suffice and will make you look like a fool). *A note on ethics*: Controversial ethical topics (abortion, euthanasia, etc.) are not normally discussed in an interview, but be very prepared for them because there's nothing worse than being blatantly ignorant of medical issues that you will most likely face as a doctor.

Some Common Interview Questions

It is usually helpful to reflect on and work out some answers to common questions you may be asked in the interview. You don't want to memorize answers (or at least not make it look like you did), but if you have never thought about some topics, it is very hard to come up with a good answers on the spot.

However, if you are given a question you don't know the answer to or you can't think of anything for a reply, you can always state that you had never thought about that before or that you don't know the answer to the question. Honesty is best. Interviewers can see through insincere responses.

Some common questions you should probably answer for yourself (or rehearse with a friend) before you go to any interview are:

1. Why medicine?

2. Why do you want to be a doctor?

3. Where do you see yourself in 10 years?

4. What are your strengths and weaknesses?

5. What do you do for relaxation?

6. How do you deal with pressure and stress?

7. What are your greatest qualities? (or your worst?)

8. If you could cure a disease, which would it be and why?

9. What is the greatest challenge facing medicine today? How would you fix it?

10. Tell me about yourself.

11. You wrote in your personal statement that....What did you learn from that?

12. Your application shows...What did you learn from that?

13. What will you do if you are not accepted? And again next year?

14. This physician says... about you in this letter. What did you do to convince him of that?

15. Tell me about your research project.

16. Tell me about your... activity.

17. What do you like to do?

18. Ask me a question now.

19. What do you see as your greatest challenge?

20. Why would you be a good physician?

21. What characteristics does a good doctor have?

22. What three things would you change about yourself?

23. Discuss your volunteer work, clinical experiences, shadowing.

24. Tell me about a life-changing experience you have had. What did you learn from it?

Ethical Questions

First, let's clarify what ethical questions are for: Interviewers want to see how you think, if you can navigate difficult scenarios. The answer you give, supporting one position or another is not as important as your reasoning. In fact, often, reasoning through both choices openly with them and stating that this is hard to resolve is the best way to go. It shows that you understand the dilemma and that you can navigate through it on both sides. What they care about is your reasoning.

Some other thoughts

Be aware of legal implications. Euthanasia (assisted suicide) is illegal in most places, for example. So, elaborating on how you would assist a patient would be a bad idea even if you support the idea in general. You may want to state "I don't know about the legal side of this issue, but assuming it would be legal, I would...". Then present your position. This shows you are thinking and would certainly obey the law.

When a tough question is asked, finding a good starting point is essential. "Hmm, let me think," and "That's tough," are acceptable time fillers, as long as you come up with an answer that reflects your added thought. If you've prepared for the question, the rest should flow naturally as you and your interviewer begin talking. On the other hand, responding immediately with a short, clichéd response tells your interviewer nothing about you as a person and gives the two of you nowhere to go except to the next question.

The interview is your time to shine, and, without being blatant about it, you should try to steer the interview in a direction that allows you to showcase the best things about you. Thoughtful and honest answers are the best way to do this.

During your interviews, also remember that you are allowed to ask the interviewer a question or two. In fact, this is encouraged, and a good interviewer will ask you if there is anything you would like to know at the end of the interview. You can impress them by stating that, yes, there are a few things you would like to know: For instance, what is the school's ideal graduate like? What are some things that this school prides itself on? The list of good questions is endless, but they should go farther than questions like, "What kind of financial aid can I get?" Questions with answers that can be found by reading materials handed out that day, or online before the interview, don't impress your interviewer. Asking good questions allows you to learn more about the school - remember, you're going to pay for your education, so they need to impress you as well - while also letting your interviewer know that you value your education, and that you've done some thinking prior to the interview. You should write these down before interview day, or during the day if you think of more, and refer back to them when asked if you have them. They will be impressed when you say that you do.

Mock Interview

Even the best need a little tune-up before the big game, and there is no bigger game than interview day. If you've had experience with interviews when applying for undergrad or for jobs, then you're a step ahead. What you should do to prepare will depend on the resources you have at your disposal, but with something as big as medical school at stake, I'd suggest using all that are available.

Ask around, and I'm sure you can find someone to give you a practice interview. Remember, you're not looking for someone to throw new questions at you; you're looking for someone to ask the generic questions that you know you'll face. Your mock interviewer is there to point out the fact that you appeared to be studying your shoes in search of an answer to the question of why you want to be a doctor, and to suggest an alternative method of presentation.

You need to think about that in advance. Try to think about your long-term goals--you might ask a question whether attending their schools will enable you to achieve them or you might ask that given what your goals are, how you would go around achieving them at that particular school. You can ask about facilities, opportunities, academics, clinical and anything else. Try not to ask questions just for the sake of asking them--people see it and do not appreciate them. On the other hand if you ask something specific and incisive it might give a good impression. This is the time to think about yourself--ask questions about your needs, wants and desires.

After your interview, you might receive an acceptance letter, a rejection letter or a letter saying you have been placed on hold. Schools vary greatly in the time they take to make and communicate decisions; you may hear nothing for quite a while.

Many medical schools begin interviewing in September and they continue to interview until all their spaces are filled. By March 15, medical schools are required to have made as many offers as they have places in the entering class.

After you receive an acceptance, you will have a certain period of time to make a decision. Consider carefully the school and its program and withdraw from schools you will not be attending. Except in certain circumstances, particularly regarding financial aid, you should not hold more than two acceptances at one time. By mid-May you should have decided on the medical school you will be attending.

Be optimistic if you are wait-listed. Many candidates move off the wait-list to acceptance during the spring and early summer.

And once again, be prepared to wait. A lot. It can take the schools even longer to reach a decision after the interview than it did for them to decide to grant you an interview.

Once again, interviews differ from school to school, but the point I'm trying to make is that, aside from the pressure you might feel while you're in the actual interview, your interview date will really be geared toward making you feel at home and impressed with the medical school you are visiting. So, just relax. Everyone else is nervous, too. And remember, they invited you to the interview because they liked you and wanted to get to know you better - they want you to succeed.

You should be able to get a good feel for the school, the faculty, the students, facilities, etc. while you are there.

That is part of the reason you are there, to help you decide if you would like to spend the next 4 years there, or not.

How much time/money do interviews cost?

An interview at a medical school close to your current residence will cost you very little money and only one-day's worth of time. Interviews at distant medical schools will cost you airfare/hotel/restaurant money (expect to pay $300-1000 dollars per distant interview), and will cost you at least two days worth of time (one day to get there, another to do the interview and come back). Remember this when making decisions regarding the schools to which you want to apply. To make the point more vivid: if you apply to 10 geographically distant schools, and get interviews to all of them, expect to miss 20 days of school and spend $3000-10,000 dollars.

How many interviewees are accepted to medical school?

Usually between 10-25% of interviewees of a particular medical school gain admission to that school.

Finally, and this is a key point, remember to save the sheet of paper that lists the names of your interviewers. You'll need to write thank-you notes, and your memory of the day might be a bit of a blur. As is the case in any part of the business world, a well written thank-you note can mean the difference between acceptance and rejection, and step one is remembering to whom the note should be sent!

Post-interview

Alright. You secured an interview, did reasonably well, and now you've got a little time to relax and enjoy senior year. While the hard work is basically over, there are just a few more things that you should know:

• Once a school decides to accept you, they'll inform you of their decision and ask you to respond in some way. This doesn't mean you have to enroll, they just want to make sure they'll be sending their promotional materials to someone who still cares to hear from them.

• You can hold on to as many acceptances as you want throughout the year, but you can only hold on to one of them after May 15. If you can find it in your heart to release your spot at a school you know you don't want to attend before May 15, please do. You'll make some other premed very happy.

• Holding on to your one spot after May 15 doesn't mean you have to send in your deposit immediately and go there. I know plenty of people who waited most of the summer to be invited to the school they really wanted to attend, and some actually got in. If you're still holding out for someplace in particular, feel free to do so.

Handling Acceptances/Wait-lists/Rejection

The three ultimate outcomes of your application to medial school are Acceptance, Rejection or a spot on the Wait List.

Normally, medical schools have to make more offers than they have spots available in their class to fill each class. This works in your favor. If a school has 100 spots to fill, they may have to extend 150, 200 or 300 offers to get 100 students to actually attend their school. If the school is very prestigious, then they typically have to extend fewer offers to fill the class. If they are the "backup" school for many applicants who would rather go elsewhere, then they have to extent more offers.

I've been accepted to a medical school; what do I do?

You will have about two weeks to respond to a school's offer of admission. Asking a school to reserve a seat in their class for you does not force you to go to that particular school. In fact, you can hold multiple acceptances simultaneously (i.e., you can reserve a seat in more than one school). If you get accepted by a school which you decide against attending, withdraw your application promptly; if you don't, you'll be depriving someone else of their chance to attend medical school.

Acceptance

Celebrate your acceptance letters! Congratulations!
You made it! All the hard work in preparation has paid off!

Of course, you want to get acceptance letters from medical schools - at least from one school. Acceptance letters are mailed within about 2 to 4 weeks from your interview date by most schools. A few schools notify students with a few days and a few schools even take several or many months to notify applicants of their decisions. A few medical schools notify most of their applicant pool at once - on a given day, rather than on a rolling basis.

You typically have until about April 15th to make your final decision of where to attend. However, you are typically only given 10 - 14 days from the day you receive the acceptance letter to make a deposit and indicate that you are interested in attending there. Once the deposit is made and you respond to the school, the medial school will hold the spot for you.

Make sure you pay your deposit and have the school hold the spot for you. This does not mean that you actually have to attend this particular school in the end. Once you have made deposits at several schools (with several offers), you can still decide where you really want to study medicine, after considering all of your options. So, by making the deposit, you don't promise or commit to attend that particular school.

For most allopathic (MD) schools, these deposits are usually only $100, but there are exceptions with higher deposit amounts. The deposits are typically refundable or will be applied towards your tuition if you attend there eventually. However, for most osteopathic (DO) schools, the deposits are between $500 and $1,000 and are most often non-refundable.

If you got accepted, good for you. Getting into med school is a major accomplishment and you should be proud of yourself. The school will generally send you a package with a whole bunch of stuff in it, and normally something you fill out that says you accept the seat in the class. Fill this out as soon as you get it or you may lose your spot. Make sure that if you've been accepted multiple places that you know when the deadline is when you can only hold one seat. After that date, you could risk losing all of your seats if you hold more than one. Start working on the financial aid package and start looking for apartments near the school. And sit back and congratulate yourself. You've started on a journey that will lead you far.

I got wait-listed; what does this mean?

The school has not accepted you, but has not rejected you either; in essence, you're in medical school limbo. Your chance of getting into medical school if wait-listed is between 1-25% depending on the school. Generally, even if you're wait-listed, you'll know by the end of May whether you've been accepted, but the school may tell you the day before classes begin.

Medical schools maintain lists of students who are qualified for admissions, but just barely didn't make the first cut to fill the class. These students are placed on the wait list, which is typically numbered, so each student is assigned a specific numbered spot on the list.

Most schools will reveal how many students, who were initially placed on the wait list, were offered spots in previous years, so you can get an idea if you really have a chance to get an offer. But there is some fluctuation. Also, some medical schools may not let you know the exact number you are on the list or how many students on the wait list where eventually offered spots in the class in previous years.

As an example, if the school typically takes 10 applicants from their wait list every year, and you're number 9 on the list this year, your chances may be good. It's no guarantee. It all depends on how many other applicants decline offers at that school late in the game that year. For sure, if you're in the top 3 or 4 on the wait list, you'll have very good chances at any school.

Being on a wait list can be good and bad. Obviously, if you don't have any other offers, a wait list spot is better than nothing. Also, you may have other offers, but your first-choice school, where you would rather study medicine, has placed you on the wait list. In this case, you can wait until you have to decide to see if your wait list spot turns into a real spot in the class.

All you have to do when that date comes around is to make a decision among the offers you have already received. So, any school which has offered you a spot in the class demands an answer of "yes" or "no". Hopefully, you have at least one offer, which you can accept at that point. This does not apply to wait lists - you can remain on different wait lists until class begins - even if you have accepted a spot at some school already.

So, even once you have told another school that you will be attending there, you can still change your mind, up to the day you actually begin class and have to pay your tuition. So, it is, in theory, possible to receive a phone call from a school notifying you that your wait list spot has turned into a real spot at some school until the day before classes start.

If you got onto the always-ambiguous wait list: don't despair, there is still hope. Make sure that you tell the school that you are interested in keeping your name on the wait list. Even though this is not an acceptance, it means that they think you deserve some extra consideration. The wait lists at most schools are active until the first day of classes, so who knows, you may get a midsummer surprise.

I was rejected by everyone; what do I do now?

Sometimes the best candidates are rejected for no apparent reason. You can take time off to get more medically-related work/volunteer experiences, or you can go to graduate school and obtain a Masters Degree/Ph.D., then reapply when your credentials are stronger. Do not reapply until you have significantly improved your credentials. Most schools have a policy of accepting a maximum of 2-3 applications from the same candidate. Also, be prepared to resubmit a new AMCAS application, secondary applications, and new letters of recommendation (note that some medical schools will allow you to use parts of your original application when applying for a second time).

Most people get some rejection letters. That's normal. It's certainly hard when the first letter you receive back is a rejection. But, don't give up. Some rejections are normal. Often, it depends on the interviewer you had that day and whether or not you connected with that person. It may have nothing to do with your application or your personality.

If you did not receive any acceptance letter at all (and you applied to a dozen or more schools), you will need to re-evaluate your options. Don't despair. This does not mean that you are not meant to be a physician. I know several individuals who applied at least two years in a row before getting accepted. For some, it even takes 3 tries.

You will need to analyze your overall application and see which areas can be improved within another year, before applying again.

If you didn't get in anywhere; don't take it personally. There are so many applicants for so few spots that tough decisions have to be made. Take a year off to do something meaningful. Do a year of post-graduate service. Get a job in a hospital working with patients somehow. Do research in a lab and get published. Or maybe you want to get a master's or PhD degree before going on to med school. Whatever you do, make sure that it is meaningful and will enhance your standing as an applicant. Most schools will allow you to apply only 2-3 times. But whatever you do, don't give up on yourself, or your dream. If you believe you can do it, then you will.

Re-Applying

Overview

Many applicants do not succeed the first year they apply. In fact, a fairly large percentage of students in each class are successful re-applicants. Generally, admissions offices look at re-application favorably since it shows commitment and persistence on your part and strengthens your position that you really want to be a physician.

There are three main reasons why you may have to re-apply:
(1) You weren't prepared sufficiently or your overall application was not strong enough.
(2) You applied to too few schools - maybe the one or two medical schools in your state only.
(3) You applied only to top schools or the wrong set of schools.

If your previous application needs improvement

There are some very important considerations before re-applying. If you have done nothing to improve your overall application since the previous year, re-applying to the same schools will do nothing for you. You have to show improvements in your application, by increasing your MCAT score, doing more research, shadowing, etc. You don't have to show improvement in each area, but overall your application should become stronger.

Spend some additional time in a medically related job, volunteer opportunity or research and do some serious research, for example. Also, if your MCAT was particularly weak, that may warrant some serious preparation and retaking the MCAT.

If you applied to too few schools or the wrong schools

Some applicants only apply to 1 or 2 schools. That's a mistake. Although some few applicants still get in by applying to only one or two schools, most are putting themselves at a serious disadvantage. An average applicant should be applying to at least a dozen schools.

Just as it is essential to apply to enough schools, it's also important to apply to the right schools. If your MCAT and other credentials (extra-curriculars, research, etc) are very good, applying to the top schools will probably be fine. Most applicants should have a good mix of schools they are applying to, including some of the less competitive schools.

So, if you're MCAT is a little lower, don't expect to get into the top schools - although you still might. Apply and re-apply accordingly. You can still include some top schools in the mix - and may well have a chance - but be sure to include mostly medical schools that take more average applicants and not just the elite applicants.

Also, consider including osteopathic schools (DO) in the mix more prominently. These typically have lower MCAT and GPA requirements, among other things. A good alternative can also be Podiatry schools if you're interested in that. Caribbean schools are also an alternative.

What If I Do Not Get Into Medical School?

By the beginning of June the majority of the movement off medical school wait lists has occurred, so that if you are not accepted to medical school by this time you will need to apply again. However, before you apply again you need to assess your application portfolio and determine why you were not accepted. When reapplying you need to have changed your portfolio for the better—otherwise, reapplication will probably result in the same outcome.

1. First, you know how competitive the application process is, so much of the reason you were not accepted is pure numbers. Some of the application process is random and unscientific, so take heart.

2. Second, look at the components of your application which include:
   GPA
   MCAT scores
   Experience in health care
   Motivation level in personal statement
   Interviewing and interpersonal skills

3. Before you reapply you should address these components of your application. The first two (numerical) elements of your application are the most important. They are what get you in the door for the interview. The last three characteristics carry you the rest of the way.

- **GPA**
  If your overall GPA (particularly your science GPA) is low, you need to take additional coursework to boost your GPA. If additional course work will slightly boost your GPA, but not above 3.4-3.5, you may want to consider applying to

osteopathic medical school the second time around, in order to enhance your chances for acceptance.

- **MCAT Scores**

    If your MCAT scores are 9's or below across the board you will need to consider retaking the exam. To do this you will need to prepare and improve your knowledge in the areas where you have the lowest scores. You may want to take additional course work to boost your knowledge, or put in extra time with MCAT preparation books or a course. If your scores do not improve the second time you take the exam you may want to consider applying to osteopathic medical school the next time around.

- **Follow-up Counseling with the Medical Schools**

    It can also be helpful to contact any schools that rejected you application, and see if they will conduct a follow-up counseling session with you regarding how your application could improve for the next application cycle. Not all medical schools will be willing to discuss your application with you but you should at least call and check. The admissions counselors and directors may want to wait till the interviewing for that year is over before they have time to truly discuss your situation, so be patient.

- **Experience in Health Care**

    If you do not have sufficient past experience in a health care environment, then the obvious course of action is to strengthen this aspect by additional volunteer or paid work. On the other hand, your experience may be sufficient but may not be apparent in your personal statement, your overall application or at your interview. If this is the case you will need to consult with the Faculty Advisor and Program Administrator to see how to improve this aspect of your profile.

- You might also want to look at Academic Record Enhancing Post-Baccalaureate Premedical Programs or getting a Master's Degree in a Molecular Biology Field in order to prove your self and be better prepared to take the MCAT a second or third time

- **Motivational Level in Personal Statement and Interview Skills**
  You may also want to schedule a mock interview through your career planning office to see if you may need to improve on your interview skills.

If you are not accepted into a medical school, hopefully, you have considered a back-up plan and can begin pursuing these goals either permanently or until you apply to medical school again.

There are many health-related occupations which may either become permanent careers or provide valuable experience in medically-related positions should you plan to re-apply. Other health-related careers which require post-graduate training include physician's assistant, nurse practitioner, pharmacist, dentist, or optometrist. In addition, there are other health-related occupations which require minimal training or certification at an undergraduate or post-graduate level including: emergency medical technician, physical therapist, occupational therapist, health care administrator, laboratory technician, and nurse.

If you are considering reapplying, make an appointment with at least one medical school admissions director for assistance in identifying weaknesses in your application. Generally, these weaknesses can be classified as academic, experiential, or personal. The key when reapplying to medical school is to have a solid response on your application when admissions members ask "what's new." They will look closely to see whether you have addressed any area of defined deficiency from your prior application.

A backup plan

Nobody likes being turned down when applying to medical school, but there are a considerable number of worthy applicants who just won't get accepted their first time around. Maybe they needed a few more points on the MCAT, or perhaps they didn't quite have the GPA to make the cut, but they were close nonetheless. They know deep down that they have what it takes to be a great doctor, and they're determined to make it into medical school one way or another. That's a great attitude to have. In fact, a close look at the AAMC's website reveals that the average age for incoming medical students is 24, which means that your average medical student didn't come straight out of undergrad. But still, when the acceptance letter never comes, it's easy to get discouraged. So, what's an applicant to do next?

Of the people I know who didn't make it into medical school on the first try, the ones who were least upset by the news were the ones who already had a backup plan in place, just in case. When you apply, you'll probably have a feeling about your chances. If you think your overall application might not be strong enough to merit acceptance from any of the schools to which you applied, it's time to start thinking about what you'll do if things don't pan out exactly as you had planned. Take heart in the fact that not everyone begins medical school fresh out of undergrad, and, in the fact, that there are plenty of things you can do to improve your chances of getting in the second time around.

The most popular backup plan among people I know has been to get a graduate degree in something science-related. These degrees usually take a year or two to complete, but they will give you extra experience to impress interviewers, new contacts for letters of recommendation (you'll need new ones for your next application), and the look of someone who is serious about becoming a doctor. Some schools even offer a program that allows people who have obtained certain graduate degrees to begin as second-year medical students at the affiliated medical school. In that case, you'll hardly lose any time at all. The key here is to make sure you don't wait until you're officially denied entry into all the schools to which you applied; start looking for jobs or grad school positions in late fall or early spring, so that you aren't caught totally off-guard if things don't go as you'd hoped.

International students face a lot of hurdles in applying to U.S. medical schools. U.S. citizens, especially residents of the state where the medical school is located will be given preference over an equally qualified international student. International students will also have to prove that they have the funds to pay outright for medical school expenses because they will not be eligible for financial aid in most cases. Studying at a school outside the U.S. is fine, but in order to practice medicine in the U.S. you will need to pass the foreign graduates medical licensing exam or the USMLE steps 1 through 3, as well as doing a residency in the U.S. I'm not trying to discourage anyone from applying, but those are the rules. Your best bet is to consult directly with any schools you may be interested in applying to and give them your specific circumstances.

Activities for a Year Off

During the glide year you will be filling out secondary applications, going to interviews, and wondering what you will be doing next year. You also need to keep your foot in the door of the medical field in order to show your continued interest and dedication. You do not need to do all of the following, but you should consider doing at least two of them in addition to applying to medical school. Do more if you are able to.

Things besides applying to medical school you should be doing:

> Take additional courses in upper division biology and/or chemistry. Particularly useful subjects include: (if you haven't had them already):
> - biochemistry
> - cell biology
> - genetics
> - molecular biology
> - neurobiology
> - physiology

> Get a job in order to support yourself, pay for application fees, finance travel to interviews, and pay off educational debts. However, if you can find work in a clinical health care area, or biological/medical research environment you may strengthen your medical school application.

If you are fortunate enough not to need to work, additional volunteer work in healthcare or research could also strengthen your application.

If you receive MCAT scores of 9 or lower you may need to retake the MCAT. This means that some of your time during the glide year should go toward studying for the MCAT or taking a review course.

Post-acceptance Plans/Financial Aid

I know where I'm going to medical school, what now?

Now you must start looking for an apartment/condo (many schools don't have on-campus housing) and provide the school with the additional financial-aid information needed to complete your request for aid. (Note that your FAFSA should be renewed by mid-February to be considered for Federal assistance. You should complete the FAFSA even if you have not yet been accepted to medical school by this time.) Since every medical school's financial aid policy is different, you must contact individual schools for more detailed financial information. Note that 99% of aid received is in the form of loans, many of which have interest rates attached to them. The average amount borrowed by medical school students is $75,000-150,000 and the average indebtedness of medical school students is $150,000-300,000 (this higher figure is due to the compounding of interest).

How do I pay for Medical School?

- Work closely with the financial aid office of the medical school you are interested in attending.
- Even if you have not yet been accepted, begin to fill out the national financial aid form (FAFSA) by February 15th of your application year. You can also take care of this electronically at http://www.fafsa.ed.gov.
- Check with every school to which you are applying, to request and/or find out about financial deadlines, their title IV codes, their in-house financial aid application instructions, and about institutional scholarships.

- Pay off your consumer debt and check your credit rating. Be careful how you use your credit cards. Consumer credit is not an investment; it is a means of improving your standard of living on a temporary basis.
- Don't live the lifestyle of a doctor until you've completed your training—get in the habit of being thrifty! If you live like a doctor while in school, you may have to live like a student when you are a doctor.
- Educate yourself about the different loans available: Stafford, Perkins, primary care, alternative, and institutional loans. What are the differences between subsidized and unsubsidized loans? What are the interest rates of the various loans you can choose from and are they adjustable? What is the grace period and can they be deferred? Do they allow for forbearance?
- Ask the financial-aid offices to use projected income. You will not be working during medical school so make sure they are taking your no income status into account when they are looking at your need. (This will also apply if a spouse is moving and quitting his/her job).
- Keep the financial aid office and your lenders up to date on any address changes during the application process. This is best done in writing.
- Explore scholarship opportunities through private organizations, foundations, and associations as well as the federal government loan programs.
- Discuss the cost of medical school with your family and determine the extent to which they plan to assist you financially.
- Provide your parent's information so you are considered for all sources of aid. (This will not affect your legibility for Federal Aid.) If there will be a reduction in parental income let the financial aid office know.
- Respond promptly to additional information requests. If you speak with counselors at the various offices keep notes on the name of the person you spoke with, the date and time you called, and the answers to the questions you asked. Make sure you have an answering machine or message service so that the financial aid office can get a hold of you.
- Keep copies and start a financial aid file. Keep copies of your and your parent's tax returns, your financial aid applications, award letters, and loan documents.

- Keep a cumulative record of your educational loans. This type of record keeping enables you to estimate your projected debt level and monthly payments.
- Confirm all of your telephone conversations with your lenders in writing via a follow-up letter. Always a sound business practice.
- If you are a non-state resident in a public school, find out how you can establish residency.

Scholarships and Funding Sources

1. **Pennies from Heaven Scholarship Guide**
2. **The National Health Service Corps. (Excerpted from the NHSC website)**

   The National Health Service Corps (NHSC) is committed to improving the health of the Nation's underserved:

   • Uniting communities in need with caring health professionals

   • Supporting communities' efforts to build better systems of care

   The NHSC provides comprehensive team-based health care that bridges geographic, financial, cultural, and language barriers. We will not stop until all Americans, everywhere; have access to quality health care, especially for health issues that have the highest racial, ethnic, and socioeconomic disparities in treatment success. HIV/AIDS, mental health, dental care, cardiovascular disease, cancer, diabetes, childhood and adult immunizations, and infant mortality are this organizations concerns.

   NHSC Scholarship Application Information Bulletin
   http://nhsc.bhpr.hrsa.gov/applications/scholar_04
   This Applicant Information Bulletin explains in detail the NHSC Scholarship program, including eligibility requirements, funding preferences, application process, benefits and service requirements. Learn more about the NHSC Scholarship Program by reading the Applicant Information Bulletin. Please note that this is not an application.
   Applications for the NHSC Scholarship Program can be obtained by calling 1-800-221-9393.

NHSC Loan Repayment Application Information Bulletin

http://nhsc.bhpr.hrsa.gov/applications/lrp_05

This Applicant Information Bulletin explains in detail the FY 2005 NHSC LRP, including eligibility requirements, funding preferences, application process, benefits and service requirements. Learn more about the NHSC Loan Repayment Program by reading the Applicant Information Bulletin. Please note that this is not an application. Applications for the NHSC LRP can be obtained by calling 1-800-221-9393.

3. **Armed Forces Health Profession Scholarship Program**

   Amount: Full tuition, fees, and monthly stipend. Stipends are subject to taxation. Required books and microscope rental fee are reimbursed. All three branches offer scholarships. Restriction: Candidates must be no more than 35 years old at graduation for the Army and Air Force; the Navy extends this age limit to age 40. Prior military time may waive this restriction - contact your recruiter.

   Repayment: One year's active service as a commissioned officer for each year of scholarship support is required. (4 year, 3 year, 2-year scholarships available). The minimum obligation is three years. The Army and Navy offer a two-year scholarship with a payback of a three-year obligation. Applications: Contact the nearest Army, Navy, or Air Force recruiting office. Our FAO offers these phone numbers for your assistance. Each branch maintains separate deadlines. Start the application process early.

   Military Representatives:

	Navy	Army	Air Force
Contact	Andrea M. DeSanto	David A. Glen	Abbey Carey
Title	Lieutenant	Captain	Technical Sergeant

Phone	(800) 252-1586 ext. 291	(626) 535-9711	(562) 435-0019
E-mail	desantoa@cnrc.navy.mil	David.Glen@usarec.army.mil	abbey.carey@rs.af.mil
Web Site	www.elnavy.com	www.goarmy.com	www.airforce.com

Time spent in residency does not count towards paying back your owed time. The Army and the Navy are even tougher than the Air force in terms of granting civilian residency deferments, and most of the time you end up doing a military internship and serving as a general medical officer for your 3 or 4 years of pay back time. If you don't mind traveling where the military sends you then it is a great life, but also consider the effects the military way of life would have on your significant other.

All three services have a medical school, the Uniformed Services School, in Bethesda Maryland, through which you serve in active duty during medical school (with full pay and benefits) and agree to pay back seven years as an M.D. after graduation. Consider this if you are thinking about a career in the military (you can retire in 20 years at half pay). With all routes you end up commissioned as an O-3 (captain in the Army or Air Force).

Other routes not in the military, include the Public Health Service and the Indian Health Service, in which you agree to work in underserved areas after your residency in a primary care field. These programs also have excellent loan repayment programs which give you more flexibility in arranging a site to practice in after residency.

What Financial Aid is available for medical students?

Here again, shouldn't you let the cost of medical education restrict your choice of medical schools. When you're accepted, the school will work with you and your family to make sure you'll be able to pay your tuition fee and living. Here are the list of loans available for medical students:

- Stafford Loan program (formerly the Guaranteed Student Loan)
- Health Education Assistance Loan (HEAL)
- Supplemental Loan for Students (SLS)
- Perkins Loan
- Homan Loan
- University Loans

You may want to consider federally-funded Armed Forces Scholarship and the Medical Scientist Training Program (MSTP) which are open to all and pay tuition plus stipend.

Financial Planning Tools

Monetary Decisions for Medical Doctors (excerpted from the AAMC website)

(MD)2 : Monetary Decisions for Medical Doctors is a comprehensive, three-part program developed by the AAMC to assist premedical and medical students in their planning for the financial aspects of their medical education. Divided into three sections—The Premedical School Years, The Medical School Years, and Residency and Early Practice Years—(MD)2 provides practical and comprehensive information specifically tailored to students throughout their medical education. This online resource contains information about making a successful transition to medical school, credit and consumer debt, types of financial aid, the financial aid application process, and relevant reference materials. Go to http://www.aamc.org/students/financing/md2/start.htm

Credit Rating

Look into your credit rating and your parents' credit rating as soon as possible. It might affect your loan applications to medical school.

Ordering a copy of your Credit Report:

Experian National
Assistance Center (formerly TRW)
P.O. Box 2104
Allen, TX 75013-2104
(888) 397-3742
http://www.experian.com
Cost $8.00 (most states)

Consumer Trans Union Corp.
Consumer Disclosure Ctr.
P.O. Box 390
Springfield, PA 19064-0390
(800) 888-4213
http://www.tuc.com
Cost $8.00 (most states)

Equifax Information Service Center
P.O. Box 74021
Atlanta, GA 30374-0241
(800) 997-2493
http://www.equifax.com
Cost $8.00 (most states)

Requests should include the following:
- First, middle and last name (include Jr., Sr., II, III)
- Current address and previous addresses for the past 5 years
- Social Security Number
- Date of Birth
- Phone Number
- Signature
- Fee (if applicable

Acknowledging your Resources

Your success or failure in getting into medical school rests on your perseverance and accomplishments, as well as support from family, faculty, and friends. Acknowledge their support and thank them for all of their assistance.

Applicants by State of Legal Residence, 1995-2006

Region	Applicants by State	1995	1996	1997	1998	1999	2000	2001	2002	2003	2004	2005	2006	Change 2005-06
Northeast	State of Legal Residence***													
	Connecticut	495	521	470	377	373	369	329	306	373	408	431	414	-3.9%
	Delaware	104	110	100	90	82	93	64	70	71	64	78	78	0.0%
	District of Columbia	122	96	87	84	71	71	78	90	76	92	81	87	7.4%
	Maine	105	104	85	75	61	62	65	53	73	73	82	84	2.4%
	Maryland	1,287	1,287	1,213	1,090	971	922	845	820	876	810	909	913	0.4%
	Massachusetts	1,094	1,208	1,038	940	944	831	762	705	776	787	867	897	3.5%
	New Hampshire	94	73	75	76	82	82	74	58	76	67	73	97	32.9%
	New Jersey	1,645	1,625	1,511	1,317	1,236	1,287	1,165	1,164	1,107	1,199	1,189	1,358	14.2%
	New York	3,953	3,917	3,413	3,167	2,891	2,779	2,542	2,494	2,630	2,601	2,706	2,702	-0.1%
	Pennsylvania	1,829	1,644	1,612	1,520	1,365	1,272	1,242	1,115	1,190	1,210	1,283	1,423	10.9%
	Rhode Island	78	89	81	85	71	66	60	62	73	79	71	80	12.7%
	Vermont	105	119	115	106	101	95	76	70	77	79	98	87	-11.2%
	All	10,911	10,993	9,800	8,927	8,248	7,909	7,302	6,945	7,404	7,409	7,867	8,220	4.5%
Central	State of Legal Residence***													
	Illinois	2,376	2,416	2,231	2,227	1,940	1,841	1,717	1,639	1,646	1,712	1,749	1,844	5.4%
	Indiana	753	772	709	667	645	597	551	563	619	620	692	702	1.4%
	Iowa	372	421	418	384	353	359	359	321	329	339	348	341	-2.0%
	Kansas	477	475	445	420	434	460	423	426	432	442	436	434	-0.5%
	Michigan	1,602	1,703	1,630	1,518	1,344	1,305	1,156	1,141	1,229	1,202	1,334	1,347	1.0%
	Minnesota	857	918	893	840	796	724	639	563	640	639	697	761	9.2%
	Missouri	734	679	611	630	604	557	438	497	464	468	567	568	0.2%
	Nebraska	399	414	410	309	338	318	277	286	283	285	303	291	-4.0%
	North Dakota	136	153	145	138	88	83	89	122	137	128	131	134	2.3%
	Ohio	1,918	1,930	1,789	1,743	1,549	1,441	1,397	1,355	1,366	1,465	1,480	1,485	0.3%
	South Dakota	120	155	144	122	131	164	148	136	114	142	153	142	-7.2%
	Wisconsin	664	655	633	681	656	611	596	588	590	672	690	680	-1.4%
	All	10,408	10,693	10,064	9,679	8,678	8,466	7,849	7,637	7,879	8,137	8,880	8,729	1.7%
South	State of Legal Residence***													
	Alabama	647	603	608	573	536	498	445	464	479	455	479	542	13.2%
	Arkansas	396	443	429	372	322	288	340	352	344	324	283	305	7.8%
	Florida	1,740	1,732	1,587	1,543	1,505	1,428	1,353	1,515	1,505	1,557	1,576	1,748	10.9%
	Georgia	1,149	1,210	1,084	1,073	955	941	912	885	956	1,086	1,141	1,154	1.1%
	Kentucky	640	586	573	553	511	502	502	472	420	435	421	412	-2.1%
	Louisiana	961	958	900	947	865	868	847	857	853	844	899	880	2.0%
	Mississippi	339	348	343	360	332	300	314	271	262	266	242	314	29.8%
	North Carolina	1,144	1,201	1,073	1,025	909	891	840	765	849	879	948	962	1.5%
	Oklahoma	509	480	437	433	341	383	378	382	321	377	406	383	-5.7%
	Puerto Rico	497	457	456	468	425	355	415	469	398	382	343	374	9.0%
	South Carolina	539	626	599	555	537	463	437	460	444	497	488	503	3.1%
	Tennessee	821	797	707	725	711	729	625	614	596	584	638	682	6.9%
	Texas	2,916	2,983	2,755	2,690	2,659	2,621	2,528	2,557	2,737	2,801	3,096	3,279	5.8%
	Virginia	1,359	1,340	1,104	1,110	1,029	915	911	828	917	919	935	913	-2.4%
	West Virginia	357	398	314	370	341	319	276	250	256	217	212	241	13.7%
	U.S. Territories and Possessions	21	26	26	23	16	10	21	19	18	18	19	14	-26.3%
	All	14,038	14,190	12,995	12,824	11,994	11,514	11,142	11,180	11,365	11,644	12,098	12,712	5.1%
West	State of Legal Residence***													
	Alaska	51	62	59	60	48	59	76	75	69	71	73	85	16.4%
	Arizona	574	623	568	559	566	539	500	491	480	502	602	574	-4.7%
	California	6,066	5,847	5,163	4,749	4,454	4,446	4,093	3,858	3,979	4,193	4,288	4,452	3.8%
	Colorado	802	814	755	698	688	649	591	575	663	627	609	646	6.1%
	Hawaii	222	234	239	215	184	206	180	171	178	195	208	214	2.9%
	Idaho	110	123	125	106	115	128	122	122	113	112	101	150	-6.8%
	Montana	118	141	114	117	120	118	109	105	101	117	108	101	-6.5%
	Nevada	215	210	178	151	179	181	160	159	170	158	187	185	-1.2%
	New Mexico	364	372	334	337	333	336	270	255	248	269	245	238	-2.9%

		423	390	397	339	319	296	297	304	343	365	387	380	-1.8%
	Oregon	423	390	397	339	319	296	297	304	343	365	387	380	-1.8%
	Utah	472	434	448	488	442	486	428	426	426	463	478	488	2.1%
	Washington	799	782	775	716	688	641	621	622	700	678	670	694	3.6%
	Wyoming	71	63	69	63	62	65	67	61	59	59	73	56	-23.3%
	All	10,287	10,095	9,224	8,598	8,198	8,148	7,514	7,224	7,529	7,799	8,069	8,243	2.2%
Non-US	State of Legal Residence***													
	Foreign	920	970	917	955	1,037	992	995	577	559	684	734	1,126	53.4%
	Unknown	22	24	16	13	88	59	58	62	55	22	25	78	212.0%
	All	942	994	933	968	1,125	1,051	1,053	639	614	686	759	1,204	58.6%
All Applicants		46,586	46,965	43,016	40,996	38,443	37,088	34,860	33,625	34,791	35,735	37,373	39,108	4.6%

Source: AAMC: Data Warehouse: Applicant Matriculant File as of 10/27/2006.

Applicants and Matriculants by State of Legal Residence, 2006

			Matriculation Status					
	Applicants by State	Applicants	Matriculated In State		Matriculated Out of State		NOT Matriculated	
			N	%	N	%	N	%
Region	State of Legal Residence***							
Northeast	Connecticut	414	77	18.6	118	28.5	219	52.9
	Delaware	78			38	48.7	40	51.3
	District of Columbia	87	15	17.2	17	19.5	55	63.2
	Maine	84			39	46.4	45	53.6
	Maryland	913	147	16.1	266	29.1	500	54.8
	Massachusetts	897	217	24.2	216	24.1	464	51.7
	New Hampshire	97	6	6.2	38	39.2	53	54.6
	New Jersey	1,358	302	22.2	363	26.7	693	51.0
	New York	2,702	883	32.7	434	16.1	1,385	51.3
	Pennsylvania	1,423	438	30.8	237	16.7	748	52.6
	Rhode Island	80	13	16.3	26	32.5	41	51.3
	Vermont	87	36	41.4	10	11.5	41	47.1
	All	8,220	2,134	26.0	1,802	21.9	4,284	52.1
Central	State of Legal Residence***							
	Illinois	1,844	627	34.0	216	11.7	1,001	54.3
	Indiana	702	240	34.2	90	12.8	372	53.0
	Iowa	341	94	27.6	43	12.6	204	59.8
	Kansas	434	150	34.6	65	15.0	219	50.5
	Michigan	1,347	394	29.3	212	15.7	741	55.0
	Minnesota	761	193	25.4	132	17.3	436	57.3
	Missouri	568	199	35.0	83	14.6	286	50.4
	Nebraska	291	111	38.1	18	6.2	162	55.7
	North Dakota	134	41	30.6	13	9.7	80	59.7
	Ohio	1,485	565	38.0	147	9.9	773	52.1
	South Dakota	142	44	31.0	28	19.7	70	49.3
	Wisconsin	680	213	31.3	104	15.3	363	53.4
	All	8,729	2,871	32.9	1,151	13.2	4,707	53.9
South	State of Legal Residence***							
	Alabama	542	226	41.7	56	10.3	260	48.0
	Arkansas	305	132	43.3	17	5.6	156	51.1
	Florida	1,748	477	27.3	247	14.1	1,024	58.6
	Georgia	1,154	315	27.3	167	14.5	672	58.2
	Kentucky	412	190	46.1	26	6.3	196	47.6
	Louisiana	866	341	38.5	58	6.5	487	55.0
	Mississippi	314	110	35.0	28	8.9	176	56.1

	North Carolina	962	270	28.1	124	12.9	568	59.0
	Oklahoma	383	140	36.6	42	11.0	201	52.5
	Puerto Rico	374	188	50.3	10	2.7	176	47.1
	South Carolina	503	210	41.7	29	5.8	264	52.5
	Tennessee	682	227	33.3	67	9.8	388	56.9
	Texas	3,279	1,160	35.4	174	5.3	1,945	59.3
	Virginia	913	241	26.4	195	21.4	477	52.2
	West Virginia	241	119	49.4	22	9.1	100	41.5
	U.S. Territories and Possessions	14			5	35.7	9	64.3
	All	12,712	4,346	34.2	1,267	10.0	7,099	55.8
West	State of Legal Residence***							
	Alaska	85			29	34.1	56	65.9
	Arizona	574	110	19.2	113	19.7	351	61.1
	California	4,452	808	18.1	1,160	26.1	2,484	55.8
	Colorado	646	117	18.1	140	21.7	389	60.2
	Hawaii	214	56	26.2	37	17.3	121	56.5
	Idaho	150			61	40.7	89	59.3
	Montana	101			50	49.5	51	50.5
	Nevada	165	49	29.7	20	12.1	96	58.2
	New Mexico	238	70	29.4	39	16.4	129	54.2
	Oregon	380	84	22.1	101	26.6	195	51.3
	Utah	488	75	15.4	149	30.5	264	54.1
	Washington	694	103	14.8	187	26.9	404	58.2
	Wyoming	56			24	42.9	32	57.1
	All	8,243	1,472	17.9	2,110	25.6	4,661	58.5
Non-US	State of Legal Residence***							
	Foreign	1,126			187	16.6	939	83.4
	Unknown	78			30	38.5	48	61.5
	All	1,204			217	18.0	987	82.0
All Applicants		39,108	10,823	27.7	6,547	16.7	21,738	55.6

Source: AAMC: Data Warehouse: Applicant Matriculant File as of 10/27/2006.

Applicants and Matriculants by School and Sex, 2006

	Applications by School 2006	Applications	Applications	Applications	Applications	Applications	Matriculants	Matriculants	Matriculants	Matriculants	Matriculants
			by instate status		by Gender			by instate status		by Gender	
		Applications	In State	Out of State	Women	Men	Matriculants	In State	Out of State	Women	Men
			%	%	%	%		%	%	%	%
School State	Medical School										
AL	Alabama	1,869	25.7	74.3	46.5	53.5	176	92.0	8.0	36.9	63.1
	South Alabama	1,018	40.2	59.8	44.5	55.5	74	86.5	13.5	47.3	52.7
AR	Arkansas	904	32.7	67.3	42.5	57.5	155	85.2	14.8	41.9	58.1
AZ	Arizona	748	71.8	28.2	49.3	50.7	110	100.0	0.0	55.5	44.5
CA	Loma Linda	3,637	47.9	52.1	46.6	53.4	176	43.8	56.3	41.5	58.5
	Southern Cal - Keck	6,308	51.9	48.1	48.0	52.0	162	69.1	30.9	50.0	50.0
	Stanford	5,980	37.7	62.3	45.2	54.8	86	43.0	57.0	55.8	44.2
	UC Davis	4,313	79.0	21.0	49.5	50.5	93	95.7	4.3	62.4	37.6
	UC Irvine	3,993	85.0	15.0	49.0	51.0	104	99.0	1.0	48.1	51.9
	UC San Diego	5,238	64.5	35.5	47.3	52.7	122	91.0	9.0	48.4	51.6
	UC San Francisco	5,609	53.0	47.0	48.6	51.4	153	84.3	15.7	53.6	46.4
	UCLA - Geffen	5,278	64.8	35.2	47.5	52.5	145	87.6	12.4	46.2	53.8
	UCLA Drew	1,739	67.7	32.3	52.7	47.3	24	95.8	4.2	50.0	50.0
CO	Colorado	2,776	21.9	78.1	46.1	53.9	155	75.5	24.5	49.7	50.3

CT	Connecticut	2,699	13.9	86.1	51.4	48.6	30	83.8	16.3	60.0	40.0
	Yale	4,563	3.7	96.3	45.6	54.4	99	10.1	89.9	49.5	50.5
DC	George Washington	11,037	0.5	99.5	50.9	49.1	177	1.7	98.3	56.5	43.5
	Georgetown	8,834	0.6	99.4	48.9	51.1	191	2.1	97.9	51.3	48.7
	Howard	4,591	0.9	99.1	56.0	44.0	118	6.8	93.2	48.3	51.7
FL	Florida	2,107	62.7	37.3	50.2	49.8	124	97.6	2.4	50.8	49.2
	Florida State	1,843	67.1	32.9	50.0	50.0	109	100.0	0.0	67.0	33.0
	Miami-Miller	3,912	34.4	65.6	47.2	52.8	176	76.7	23.3	44.3	55.7
	South Florida	1,954	68.4	31.6	51.5	48.5	120	93.3	6.7	55.0	45.0
GA	Emory	5,573	10.2	89.8	51.1	48.9	114	32.5	67.5	54.4	45.6
	Georgia	1,861	51.4	48.6	52.4	47.6	190	97.4	2.6	50.0	50.0
	Mercer	896	100.0		54.3	45.7	60	100.0		48.3	51.7
	Morehouse	2,973	13.4	86.6	56.9	43.1	53	62.3	37.7	60.4	39.6
HI	Hawaii - Burns	1,629	12.2	87.8	45.6	54.4	62	90.3	9.7	50.0	50.0
IA	Iowa - Carver	2,575	12.2	87.8	44.2	55.8	142	66.2	33.8	58.5	41.5
IL	Chicago - Pritzker	7,455	12.9	87.1	47.5	52.5	106	29.2	70.8	50.9	49.1
	Chicago Med-Rosalind Franklin	7,210	14.0	86.0	48.1	51.9	185	38.4	61.6	38.9	61.1
	Illinois	5,755	28.6	71.4	48.2	51.8	324	74.4	25.6	50.0	50.0
	Loyola - Stritch	8,189	16.3	83.7	48.4	51.6	140	44.3	55.7	50.0	50.0
	Northwestern - Feinberg	6,753	13.8	86.2	47.8	52.2	174	28.7	71.3	50.0	50.0
	Rush	4,631	29.2	70.8	49.9	50.1	140	71.4	28.6	52.9	47.1
	Southern Illinois	1,097	94.8	5.2	51.9	48.1	72	100.0	0.0	54.2	45.8
IN	Indiana	2,896	23.2	76.8	46.2	53.8	280	85.7	14.3	42.5	57.5
KS	Kansas	1,685	23.9	76.1	43.7	56.3	175	85.7	14.3	48.0	52.0
KY	Kentucky	1,350	26.8	73.2	43.8	56.2	103	72.8	27.2	39.8	60.2
	Louisville	1,805	19.4	80.6	43.4	56.6	149	77.2	22.8	43.0	57.0
LA	LSU New Orleans	991	79.0	21.0	46.6	53.4	169	97.0	3.0	40.2	59.8
	LSU Shreveport	1,023	68.4	31.6	43.5	56.5	118	100.0	0.0	43.2	56.8
	Tulane	7,106	8.1	91.9	47.8	52.2	165	35.8	64.2	38.8	61.2
MA	Boston	10,032	6.9	93.1	51.2	48.8	179	15.6	84.4	54.7	45.3
	Harvard	5,950	7.0	93.0	44.4	55.6	165	7.9	92.1	53.3	46.7
	Massachusetts	763	91.0	9.0	53.9	46.1	103	97.1	2.9	59.2	40.8
	Tufts	8,573	8.1	91.9	50.8	49.2	171	44.4	55.6	43.9	56.1
MD	Johns Hopkins	5,842	7.2	92.8	45.9	54.1	120	8.3	91.7	42.5	57.5
	Maryland	4,167	18.6	81.4	51.2	48.8	160	77.5	22.5	61.9	38.1
	Uniformed Services-Hebert	1,674	6.5	93.5	32.4	67.6	172	7.6	92.4	24.4	75.6
MI	Michigan	4,781	18.5	81.5	45.0	55.0	170	45.3	54.7	50.6	49.4
	Michigan State	3,941	25.8	74.2	45.0	55.0	106	82.1	17.9	53.8	46.2
	Wayne State	3,386	34.7	65.3	46.7	53.3	288	79.9	20.1	50.7	49.3
MN	Mayo	2,869	11.4	88.6	42.8	57.2	43	27.9	72.1	48.8	51.2
	Minnesota Duluth	1,258	36.2	63.8	43.5	56.5	56	89.3	10.7	50.0	50.0
	Minnesota Twin Cities	2,494	26.2	73.8	45.7	54.3	165	79.4	20.6	49.1	50.9
MO	Missouri Columbia	916	44.8	55.2	44.1	55.9	95	83.2	16.8	44.2	55.8
	Missouri Kansas City[3]	99	62.6	37.4	59.6	40.4	99	62.6	37.4	59.6	40.4
	St Louis	5,627	6.4	93.6	44.0	56.0	176	25.0	75.0	39.8	60.2
	Washington U St Louis	4,064	4.6	95.4	44.0	56.0	122	11.5	88.5	50.0	50.0
MS	Mississippi	281	99.6	0.4	48.0	52.0	110	100.0	0.0	50.9	49.1
NC	Duke	5,166	6.8	93.2	44.6	55.4	98	7.1	92.9	51.0	49.0
	East Carolina - Brody	765	100.0		49.0	51.0	72	100.0		48.6	51.4
	North Carolina	3,615	22.7	77.3	49.4	50.6	161	89.4	10.6	45.3	54.7
	Wake Forest	6,672	9.4	90.6	46.3	53.7	114	41.2	58.8	42.1	57.9
ND	North Dakota	264	46.2	53.8	51.1	48.9	62	66.1	33.9	50.0	50.0
NE	Creighton	4,884	4.0	96.0	43.3	56.7	126	11.1	88.9	50.0	50.0
	Nebraska	1,225	22.6	77.4	44.4	55.6	118	82.2	17.8	44.1	55.9
NH	Dartmouth	4,620	1.5	98.5	47.0	53.0	82	7.3	92.7	43.9	56.1
NJ	UMDNJ - RW Johnson	3,170	35.5	64.5	50.8	49.2	165	89.1	10.9	53.3	46.7
	UMDNJ New Jersey	4,244	26.5	73.5	51.9	48.1	170	91.2	8.8	44.1	55.9

NM	New Mexico	1,157	19.3	80.7	45.3	54.7	75	93.3	6.7	48.0	52.0
NV	Nevada	997	15.5	84.5	43.1	56.9	57	86.0	14.0	50.9	49.1
NY	Albany	7,189	19.7	80.3	48.3	51.7	135	36.3	63.7	54.1	45.9
	Buffalo	3,066	51.2	48.8	48.2	51.8	140	80.7	19.3	48.6	51.4
	Columbia	6,215	16.2	83.8	47.4	52.6	155	29.0	71.0	45.8	54.2
	Cornell - Weill	5,235	20.5	79.5	47.0	53.0	101	35.6	64.4	49.5	50.5
	Einstein	6,445	22.3	77.7	48.7	51.3	183	50.8	49.2	52.5	47.5
	Mount Sinai	6,250	23.4	76.6	51.7	48.3	124	41.1	58.9	54.8	45.2
	New York Medical	9,517	17.9	82.1	49.2	50.8	194	29.9	70.1	54.1	45.9
	New York University	7,423	18.7	81.3	50.1	49.9	160	38.1	61.9	52.5	47.5
	Rochester	3,981	24.7	75.3	48.3	51.7	101	36.6	63.4	49.5	50.5
	SUNY Downstate	3,916	51.5	48.5	52.1	47.9	185	76.8	23.2	49.2	50.8
	SUNY Upstate	3,668	46.6	53.4	48.6	51.4	152	63.8	36.2	55.9	44.1
	Stony Brook	3,093	63.2	36.8	50.5	49.8	103	93.5	6.5	46.3	53.7
OH	Case Western	5,295	14.5	85.5	45.4	54.6	170	21.8	78.2	42.4	57.6
	Cincinnati	3,846	28.6	71.4	45.0	55.0	158	72.8	27.2	42.4	57.6
	Northeastern Ohio	1,627	43.5	56.6	44.8	55.2	117	95.7	4.3	55.6	44.4
	Ohio State	4,074	26.3	73.7	41.7	58.3	211	54.5	45.5	45.5	54.6
	Toledo	2,844	33.4	66.6	43.8	56.2	155	62.6	37.4	47.1	52.9
	Wright State - Boonshoft	2,765	34.2	65.8	47.5	52.5	100	89.0	11.0	65.0	35.0
OK	Oklahoma	1,075	33.2	66.8	43.3	56.7	158	88.6	11.4	38.0	62.0
OR	Oregon	3,940	8.7	91.3	47.4	52.6	120	70.0	30.0	53.3	46.7
PA	Drexel	10,501	9.9	90.1	50.0	50.0	255	28.6	71.4	49.8	50.2
	Jefferson	7,762	13.2	86.8	50.0	50.0	255	43.8	56.1	56.1	43.9
	Penn State	5,856	17.2	82.8	48.6	51.4	152	48.0	52.0	48.0	52.0
	Pennsylvania	5,730	11.5	88.5	47.9	52.1	151	27.8	72.2	47.7	52.3
	Pittsburgh	5,237	16.3	83.7	46.4	53.6	147	31.3	68.7	41.5	58.5
	Temple	8,296	12.5	87.5	50.6	49.4	175	52.6	47.4	49.1	50.9
PR	Caribe	1,039	27.1	72.9	48.0	52.0	63	76.2	23.8	42.9	57.1
	Ponce	804	39.1	60.9	51.9	48.1	68	60.6	39.4	48.5	51.5
	Puerto Rico	286	100.0		52.1	47.9	100	100.0	.	52.0	48.0
RI	Brown	4,151	1.5	98.5	47.8	52.2	91	14.3	85.7	49.5	50.5
SC	MU South Carolina	1,679	27.6	72.4	46.7	53.3	150	90.7	9.3	44.7	55.3
	South Carolina	1,712	22.7	77.3	46.4	53.6	80	92.5	7.5	40.0	60.0
SD	South Dakota	821	16.6	83.4	44.0	56.0	51	86.3	13.7	47.1	52.9
TN	East Tennessee - Quillen	1,225	39.3	60.7	44.1	55.9	60	83.3	16.7	41.7	58.3
	Meharry	3,936	6.0	94.0	55.1	44.9	93	19.4	80.6	64.5	35.5
	Tennessee	1,244	46.2	53.8	45.3	54.7	150	95.3	4.7	38.0	62.0
	Vanderbilt	4,373	7.0	93.0	45.2	54.8	106	15.1	84.9	46.2	53.8
TX	Baylor	4,326	32.2	67.8	46.7	53.3	168	75.6	24.4	48.2	51.8
	Texas A & M	2,909	85.7	14.3	49.6	50.4	85	94.1	5.9	54.1	45.9
	Texas Tech	2,856	86.7	13.3	48.6	51.4	140	95.7	4.3	43.6	56.4
	UT Galveston	3,439	83.0	17.0	49.0	51.0	229	93.0	7.0	49.3	50.7
	UT Houston	3,520	81.4	18.6	49.4	50.6	226	92.9	7.1	44.7	55.3
	UT San Antonio	3,459	83.1	16.9	49.3	50.7	220	88.2	11.8	58.2	41.8
	UT Southwestern	3,370	79.3	20.7	49.4	50.6	228	88.6	11.4	47.6	52.3
UT	Utah	1,189	36.1	63.9	30.9	69.1	102	73.5	26.5	36.3	63.7
VA	Eastern Virginia	4,234	16.1	83.9	48.5	51.5	110	64.5	35.5	44.5	55.5
	Virginia	3,722	17.9	82.1	47.5	52.5	140	47.1	52.9	44.3	55.7
	Virginia Commonwealth	4,775	14.9	85.1	48.2	51.8	184	56.5	43.5	50.5	49.5
VT	Vermont	5,440	1.6	98.4	48.3	51.7	107	33.6	66.4	57.9	42.1
WA	U Washington	3,775	17.1	82.9	46.6	53.4	182	56.6	43.4	55.5	44.5
WI	MC Wisconsin	5,752	9.6	90.4	42.8	57.2	204	47.5	52.5	50.0	50.0
	Wisconsin	2,974	19.8	80.2	44.6	55.4	150	77.3	22.7	48.0	52.0
WV	Marshall - Edwards	1,573	12.6	87.4	43.0	57.0	64	75.0	25.0	42.2	57.8
	West Virginia	2,037	10.1	89.9	44.2	55.8	109	65.1	34.9	30.3	69.7
Totals		483,148	24.7	75.3	47.9	52.1	17,370	62.3	37.7	48.6	51.4

Source: AAMC: Data Warehouse: Applicant Matriculant File as of 11/7/2006.

1. 153 Matriculants include 12 to Berkeley/UCSF joint program.
2. 145 Matriculants include 24 to UC Riverside-Haider.
3. Special 6 year undergraduate/MD program at UMKC.
4. 483,148 is the number of applications from 39,108 applicants, an average of 12 applications per applicant.

Applicants by Race and Ethnicity within Sex, 2003 - 2006

Race and Hispanic Origin of Applicants 2003 - 2006		2003 Hispanic or Not*			2004 Hispanic or Not*			2005 Hispanic or Not*			2006 Hispanic or Not*		
		N	Y	Total	N	Y	Total	N	Y	Total	N	Y	Total
Women	American Indian or Alaska Native	35	7	42	47	22	69	45	13	58	74	22	96
	American Indian or Alaska Native, Black or African American	26	2	28	28	4	32	34	4	38	17	2	19
	American Indian or Alaska Native, White	108	4	112	91	12	103	106	16	122	60	15	75
	Asian	3,093	43	3,136	3,429	50	3,479	3,699	56	3,755	3,798	49	3,847
	Asian, White	266	9	275	324	10	334	341	16	357	297	11	308
	Black or African American	1,906	22	1,928	1,940	65	2,005	1,917	68	1,985	2,007	61	2,068
	Black or African American, White	42	13	55	54	24	78	51	26	77	35	20	55
	Native Hawaiian or Other Pacific Islander	13	3	16	23	7	30	23	3	26	64	11	75
	White	9,749	600	10,349	10,017	767	10,784	10,143	889	11,032	10,373	846	11,219
	White, Other	116	67	183	7	12	19	1	2	3	3	2	5
	Other	280	436	716	43	205	248	20	63	83	40	37	77
	Unknown	86	52	138	96	122	218	140	238	378	209	353	562
	Non U.S. Citizen/Permanent Resident	497		497	516		516	627		627	794		794
	Multiple Race, N<300	158	39	197	87	16	103	74	11	85	74	19	93
	Total for Women	16,375	1,297	17,672	16,702	1,316	18,018	17,221	1,405	18,626	17,645	1,448	19,293
Men	American Indian or Alaska Native	50	10	60	60	12	72	50	17	67	72	19	91
	American Indian or Alaska Native, Black or African American	11	1	12	16	2	18	11	2	13	4		4
	American Indian or Alaska Native, White	80	9	89	115	14	129	109	18	127	79	15	94
	Asian	3,060	25	3,085	3,306	44	3,350	3,596	55	3,651	3,734	35	3,769
	Asian, White	223	6	229	278	7	285	302	12	314	271	11	282
	Black or African American	835	21	856	862	38	900	893	31	924	899	41	940
	Black or African American, White	25	10	35	37	27	64	30	16	46	20	6	26
	Native Hawaiian or Other Pacific Islander	10	6	16	16	9	25	19	5	24	47	8	55
	White	10,487	522	11,009	11,028	717	11,745	11,612	813	12,425	12,296	783	13,079
	White, Other	159	59	218	5	12	17	1	3	4	1		1
	Other	328	422	750	67	174	241	30	71	101	44	40	84
	Unknown	81	67	148	125	160	285	137	249	386	228	351	579
	Non U.S. Citizen/Permanent Resident	462		462	510		510	578		578	733		733

	Multiple Race, N<300	115	35	150	62	14	76	74	13	87	64	14	78
	Total for Men	15,926	1,193	17,119	16,487	1,230	17,717	17,442	1,305	18,747	18,492	1,323	19,815
All Applicants	American Indian or Alaska Native	85	17	102	107	34	141	95	30	125	146	41	187
	American Indian or Alaska Native, Black or African American	37	3	40	44	6	50	45	6	51	21	2	23
	American Indian or Alaska Native, White	188	13	201	206	26	232	215	34	249	139	30	169
	Asian	6,153	68	6,221	6,735	94	6,829	7,295	111	7,406	7,532	84	7,616
	Asian, White	489	15	504	602	17	619	643	28	671	568	22	590
	Black or African American	2,741	43	2,784	2,802	103	2,905	2,810	99	2,909	2,906	102	3,008
	Black or African American, White	67	23	90	91	51	142	81	42	123	55	26	81
	Native Hawaiian or Other Pacific Islander	23	9	32	39	16	55	42	8	50	111	19	130
	White	20,236	1,122	21,358	21,045	1,484	22,529	21,755	1,702	23,457	22,669	1,629	24,298
	White, Other	275	126	401	12	24	36	2	5	7	4	2	6
	Other	608	858	1,466	110	379	489	50	134	184	84	77	161
	Unknown	167	119	286	221	282	503	277	487	764	437	704	1,141
	Non U.S. Citizen/Permanent Resident	959		959	1,026		1,026	1,205		1,205	1,527		1,527
	Multiple Race, N<300	273	74	347	149	30	179	148	24	172	138	33	171
	Total for Women and Men	32,301	2,490	34,791	33,189	2,546	35,735	34,663	2,710	37,373	36,337	2,771	39,108
Total		32,301	2,490	34,791	33,189	2,546	35,735	34,663	2,710	37,373	36,337	2,771	39,108

Source: AAMC: Data Warehouse: Applicant Matriculant File as of 10/27/2006.

Applicants, Accepted Applicants, and Matriculants by Sex, 1995-2006

Data from 1995 to 2006			1995	1996	1997	1998	1999	2000	2001	2002	2003	2004	2005	2006	Change 2005-06
Applicants	Women	N	19,776	20,028	18,271	17,785	17,395	17,273	16,718	16,556	17,672	18,018	18,626	19,293	3.6%
		%	42.5	42.6	42.5	43.4	45.2	46.6	48	49.2	50.8	50.4	49.8	49.3	-0.5
	Men	N	26,810	26,937	24,745	23,211	21,048	19,815	18,142	17,069	17,119	17,717	18,747	19,815	5.7%
		%	57.5	57.4	57.5	56.6	54.8	53.4	52	50.8	49.2	49.6	50.2	50.7	0.5
Total Applicants			46,586	46,965	43,016	40,996	38,443	37,088	34,860	33,625	34,791	35,735	37,373	39,108	4.6%
First Time Applicants	Women	N	13,980	13,779	12,698	12,494	12,468	12,480	12,356	12,648	13,730	13,932	14,358	14,904	3.8%
		%	44.1	43.9	44.4	45.4	47.7	48.5	49.6	50.8	52.5	51.2	50.7	50.4	-0.3
	Men	N	17,717	17,598	15,929	15,040	13,658	13,277	12,557	12,238	12,431	13,257	13,934	14,679	5.3%
		%	55.9	56.1	55.6	54.6	52.3	51.5	50.4	49.2	47.5	48.8	49.3	49.6	0.3
Total First Time Applicants			31,697	31,377	28,627	27,534	26,126	25,757	24,913	24,886	26,161	27,189	28,292	29,583	4.6%
Acceptees	Women	N	7,437	7,439	7,484	7,685	7,966	8,027	8,294	8,631	8,732	8,768	8,766	8,959	2.2%
		%	42.8	42.8	43.2	44.2	45.7	45.8	47.5	49.1	49.8	49.6	48.7	48.6	-0.1
	Men	N	9,919	9,946	9,828	9,688	9,455	9,508	9,160	8,962	8,810	8,894	9,221	9,483	2.8%
		%	57.2	57.2	56.8	55.8	54.3	54.2	52.5	50.9	50.2	50.4	51.3	51.4	0.1
Total Acceptees			17,356	17,385	17,312	17,373	17,421	17,535	17,454	17,593	17,542	17,662	17,987	18,442	2.5%
Matriculants	Women	N	6,941	6,918	6,994	7,162	7,412	7,472	7,784	8,113	8,212	8,236	8,239	8,445	2.5%
		%	42.7	42.7	43.3	44.3	45.7	45.8	47.6	49.2	49.6	49.5	48.5	48.6	0.1
	Men	N	9,311	9,283	9,170	9,008	8,809	8,829	8,581	8,375	8,329	8,413	8,764	8,925	1.8%
		%	57.3	57.3	56.7	55.7	54.3	54.2	52.4	50.8	50.4	50.5	51.5	51.4	-0.1

Source: AAMC: Data Warehouse: Applicant Matriculant File as of 10/27/2006.

Matriculants by Race and Ethnicity within Sex, 2003 - 2006

Race and Hispanic Origin of Matriculants 2003 - 2006		2003 Hispanic or Not*		2003 Total	2004 Hispanic or Not*		2004 Total	2005 Hispanic or Not*		2005 Total	2006 Hispanic or Not*		2006 Total
		N	Y		N	Y		N	Y		N	Y	
Women	American Indian or Alaska Native	16	2	18	24	8	32	13	3	16	35	7	42
	American Indian or Alaska Native, Black or African American	6		6	7	2	9	12	1	13	5	1	6
	American Indian or Alaska Native, White	54	2	56	45	5	50	48	6	54	27	5	32
	Asian	1,545	11	1,556	1,589	15	1,604	1,658	21	1,679	1,633	16	1,649
	Asian, White	139	5	144	146	2	148	174	10	184	171	7	178
	Black or African American	700	10	710	718	20	738	665	22	687	760	15	775
	Black or African American, White	25	7	32	32	14	46	34	17	51	13	7	20
	Native Hawaiian or Other Pacific Islander	2		2	7	2	9	6	1	7	17	5	22
	White	4,779	284	5,063	4,867	351	5,218	4,713	401	5,114	4,818	397	5,215
	White, Other	53	30	83	1	7	8	1	1	2	2		2
	Other	90	176	266	12	88	100	9	32	41	11	17	28
	Unknown	62	21	83	66	54	120	109	101	210	145	156	301
	Non U.S. Citizen/Permanent Resident	110		110	110		110	146		146	143		143
	Multiple Race, N<300	69	14	83	37	6	43	32	3	35	24	8	32
	Total for Women	7,650	562	8,212	7,661	574	8,235	7,620	619	8,239	7,804	641	8,445
Men	American Indian or Alaska Native	19	3	22	24	6	30	20	7	27	33	9	42
	American Indian	5		5	5		5	5		5	2		2

	or Alaska Native, Black or African American												
	American Indian or Alaska Native, White	38	3	41	46	8	54	53	6	59	34	7	41
	Asian	1,519	11	1,530	1,505	15	1,520	1,655	17	1,672	1,609	14	1,623
	Asian, White	121	6	127	129	4	133	129	5	134	133	8	141
	Black or African American	360	8	368	368	20	388	403	13	416	395	17	412
	Black or African American, White	15	6	21	21	17	38	17	12	29	8	4	12
	Native Hawaiian or Other Pacific Islander	3	2	5	4	1	5	12	2	14	16	3	19
	White	5,345	234	5,579	5,476	342	5,818	5,582	423	6,005	5,723	376	6,099
	White, Other	57	30	87	3	4	7		1	1			
	Other	117	186	303	26	96	122	10	30	40	12	16	28
	Unknown	54	26	80	68	82	150	81	128	209	131	183	314
	Non U.S. Citizen/Permanent Resident	102		102	111		111	117		117	154		154
	Multiple Race, N<300	45	14	59	26	6	32	30	6	36	33	5	38
	Total for Men	7,800	529	8,329	7,812	601	8,413	8,114	650	8,764	8,283	642	8,925
All Matriculants	American Indian or Alaska Native	35	5	40	48	14	62	33	10	43	68	16	84
	American Indian or Alaska Native, Black or African American	11		11	12	2	14	17	1	18	7	1	8
	American Indian or Alaska Native, White	92	5	97	91	13	104	101	12	113	61	12	73
	Asian	3,064	22	3,086	3,094	30	3,124	3,313	38	3,351	3,242	30	3,272
	Asian, White	260	11	271	275	6	281	303	15	318	304	15	319
	Black or African American	1,060	18	1,078	1,086	40	1,126	1,065	35	1,103	1,155	32	1,187
	Black or African American, White	40	13	53	53	31	84	51	29	80	21	11	32
	Native Hawaiian or Other Pacific Islander	5	2	7	11	3	14	18	3	21	33	8	41
	White	10,124	518	10,642	10,343	693	11,036	10,295	824	11,119	10,541	773	11,314

White, Other	110	60	170	4	11	15	1	2	3	2		2
Other	207	362	569	38	184	222	19	62	81	23	33	56
Unknown	116	47	163	134	136	270	190	229	419	276	339	615
Non U.S. Citizen/Permanent Resident	212		212	221		221	263		263	297		297
Multiple Race, N<300	114	28	142	63	12	75	62	9	71	57	13	70
Total for Women and Men	15,450	1,091	16,541	15,473	1,175	16,648	15,734	1,269	17,003	16,087	1,283	17,370
Total	15,450	1,091	16,541	15,473	1,175	16,648	15,734	1,269	17,003	16,087	1,283	17,370

* Not Hispanic includes those designating themselves as Not Hispanic, those who did not respond to the ethnicity question, and Non U.S. Citizen/Permanent Residents.

Source: AAMC: Data Warehouse: Applicant Matriculant File as of 10/27/2006.

MCAT Scores and GPAs for Applicants and Matriculants, 1995-2006

Applicants		Application Year											
		1995	1996	1997	1998	1999	2000	2001	2002	2003	2004	2005	2006
MCAT VR	Mean	8.5	8.5	8.6	8.6	8.7	8.7	8.6	8.7	8.8	8.9	8.9	9.0
	SD	2.2	2.3	2.2	2.2	2.1	2.2	2.2	2.2	2.1	2.2	2.2	2.2
MCAT PS	Mean	8.6	8.7	8.7	8.9	9.0	8.9	9.0	9.1	9.0	9.0	9.1	9.1
	SD	2.2	2.3	2.2	2.3	2.2	2.3	2.2	2.2	2.2	2.2	2.2	2.2
MCAT BS	Mean	8.7	8.9	9.1	9.2	9.3	9.3	9.2	9.3	9.3	9.4	9.5	9.5
	SD	2.2	2.2	2.1	2.1	2.1	2.1	2.1	2.1	2.1	2.1	2.1	2.1
MCAT WS	Median	O	O	O	O	P	P	P	P	P	O	P	O
GPA science	Mean	3.22	3.26	3.30	3.32	3.34	3.35	3.36	3.36	3.36	3.36	3.37	3.38
	SD	0.49	0.48	0.47	0.47	0.46	0.46	0.46	0.46	0.46	0.46	0.45	0.45
GPA non-science	Mean	3.43	3.46	3.50	3.52	3.55	3.56	3.58	3.59	3.60	3.60	3.60	3.61
	SD	0.39	0.38	0.37	0.36	0.35	0.35	0.34	0.34	0.33	0.32	0.32	0.32
GPA total	Mean	3.31	3.34	3.38	3.40	3.43	3.44	3.45	3.46	3.47	3.47	3.48	3.48
	SD	0.41	0.40	0.39	0.38	0.38	0.38	0.38	0.37	0.37	0.37	0.36	0.36
Total Applicants		46,586	46,965	43,016	40,996	38,443	37,088	34,860	33,625	34,791	35,735	37,373	39,108

Matriculants		Application Year											
		1995	1996	1997	1998	1999	2000	2001	2002	2003	2004	2005	2006
MCAT VR	Mean	9.5	9.6	9.6	9.5	9.5	9.5	9.5	9.5	9.5	9.7	9.7	9.8
	SD	1.8	1.8	1.7	1.7	1.7	1.8	1.8	1.8	1.7	1.7	1.8	1.7
MCAT PS	Mean	9.7	9.8	9.8	9.9	10.0	10.0	10.0	10.0	9.9	9.9	10.1	10.1
	SD	2.0	2.0	2.0	2.0	1.9	2.0	1.9	1.9	1.9	1.9	1.9	1.9
MCAT BS	Mean	9.9	10.0	10.1	10.2	10.2	10.2	10.1	10.2	10.2	10.3	10.4	10.5
	SD	1.8	1.8	1.7	1.7	1.7	1.7	1.7	1.6	1.6	1.6	1.6	1.6
MCAT WS	Median	P	P	P	P	P	P	P	P	P	P	P	P
GPA science	Mean	3.47	3.50	3.52	3.52	3.53	3.54	3.54	3.54	3.55	3.56	3.56	3.57

SD	0.39	0.38	0.37	0.37	0.36	0.35	0.35	0.36	0.35	0.35	0.35	0.34
GPA non-science Mean	3.58	3.60	3.63	3.64	3.66	3.67	3.68	3.69	3.70	3.70	3.70	3.71
SD	0.32	0.32	0.31	0.30	0.30	0.29	0.28	0.27	0.26	0.26	0.26	0.26
GPA total Mean	3.52	3.54	3.56	3.57	3.59	3.60	3.60	3.61	3.62	3.62	3.63	3.64
SD	0.33	0.32	0.31	0.31	0.30	0.30	0.29	0.29	0.28	0.28	0.28	0.27
Total Matriculants	16,252	16,201	16,164	16,170	16,221	16,301	16,365	16,488	16,541	16,648	17,003	17,370

Source: AAMC: Data Warehouse: Applicant Matriculant File as of 10/27/2006.

MCAT Scores and GPAs for Applicants by State of Legal Residence, 2006

Applicants 2006	MCAT VR		MCAT PS		MCAT BS		MCAT WS			GPA science		GPA non-science		GPA total		Total
	Mean	SD	Mean	SD	Mean	SD	25th%ile	Median	75th	Mean	SD	Mean	SD	Mean	SD	
U.S. State of Legal Residence***																
Alabama	9.0	2.1	8.7	2.2	9.1	2.0	M	O	Q	3.42	0.44	3.67	0.31	3.53	0.36	542
Alaska	9.0	1.7	9.1	1.9	9.0	1.9	N	P	Q	3.37	0.41	3.63	0.32	3.48	0.34	85
Arizona	8.8	2.2	8.6	2.1	9.1	2.0	N	P	Q	3.34	0.47	3.62	0.34	3.47	0.37	574
Arkansas	8.7	2.2	7.9	2.0	8.8	2.0	M	P	Q	3.38	0.48	3.67	0.32	3.52	0.36	308
California	9.1	2.2	9.8	2.2	10.1	2.1	N	P	Q	3.34	0.45	3.57	0.31	3.44	0.36	4,452
Colorado	9.4	2.0	9.3	2.0	9.8	1.9	N	P	Q	3.43	0.42	3.61	0.34	3.51	0.33	648
Connecticut	9.5	2.0	9.4	2.0	10.0	1.8	O	O	Q	3.38	0.36	3.60	0.27	3.48	0.30	414
Delaware	8.6	2.5	8.6	2.8	9.1	2.6	M	O	Q	3.33	0.48	3.60	0.33	3.44	0.41	78
District of Columbia	8.4	2.7	8.3	2.4	8.8	2.3	N	O	Q	3.18	0.59	3.42	0.44	3.30	0.50	87
Florida	8.6	2.3	8.5	2.1	9.0	2.1	M	O	Q	3.34	0.47	3.63	0.33	3.47	0.38	1,748
Georgia	8.6	2.2	8.4	2.3	8.9	2.4	M	O	Q	3.32	0.47	3.58	0.33	3.44	0.37	1,154
Hawaii	8.5	2.1	8.7	2.3	9.2	2.1	N	O	Q	3.28	0.53	3.58	0.33	3.43	0.39	214
Idaho	9.3	1.8	9.2	2.0	9.7	1.7	M	O	Q	3.47	0.42	3.69	0.28	3.57	0.33	150
Illinois	9.0	2.1	9.1	2.2	9.4	2.0	N	O	Q	3.34	0.46	3.59	0.35	3.45	0.37	1,844
Indiana	9.2	1.9	9.1	2.0	9.5	1.9	N	O	Q	3.46	0.43	3.70	0.27	3.57	0.33	702
Iowa	9.5	1.9	9.3	2.1	9.9	1.8	N	O	Q	3.50	0.39	3.73	0.25	3.60	0.31	341
Kansas	8.8	2.1	8.5	2.0	9.0	1.9	M	O	Q	3.46	0.43	3.69	0.30	3.57	0.34	434
Kentucky	8.8	2.0	8.4	2.2	8.9	2.2	N	O	Q	3.39	0.45	3.68	0.33	3.51	0.36	412
Louisiana	8.5	2.0	8.3	2.0	8.8	2.0	M	O	Q	3.41	0.44	3.66	0.32	3.52	0.36	886
Maine	9.4	1.8	9.1	2.4	9.6	2.0	N	P	Q	3.45	0.40	3.63	0.27	3.53	0.31	84
Maryland	8.9	2.4	9.1	2.6	9.6	2.3	N	O	Q	3.34	0.46	3.60	0.33	3.45	0.36	913
Massachusetts	9.5	2.1	9.6	2.3	10.1	2.0	O	P	Q	3.36	0.44	3.55	0.33	3.44	0.36	897
Michigan	8.9	2.1	9.3	2.3	9.7	2.1	N	O	Q	3.37	0.47	3.61	0.32	3.48	0.33	1,347
Minnesota	9.3	2.0	9.4	2.0	9.7	1.9	N	P	Q	3.42	0.42	3.64	0.30	3.52	0.33	761
Mississippi	8.6	2.2	7.8	2.1	8.4	2.2	M	N	P	3.42	0.49	3.69	0.32	3.54	0.38	314
Missouri	9.2	2.1	9.0	2.2	9.5	2.0	N	P	Q	3.49	0.41	3.67	0.33	3.57	0.36	568
Montana	9.4	1.8	9.0	1.7	9.8	1.6	N	O	Q	3.51	0.37	3.71	0.26	3.60	0.30	101
Nebraska	8.8	2.0	8.5	1.9	9.0	1.9	M	O	Q	3.47	0.42	3.69	0.30	3.57	0.33	291
Nevada	8.4	2.2	8.3	2.2	9.0	2.4	M	O	Q	3.26	0.53	3.57	0.37	3.40	0.41	165
New Hampshire	9.7	2.2	9.0	2.2	9.8	2.0	O	P	Q	3.47	0.41	3.60	0.35	3.53	0.36	97
New Jersey	9.0	2.1	9.4	2.2	9.8	2.0	N	P	Q	3.39	0.45	3.58	0.31	3.48	0.33	1,356
New Mexico	9.1	2.1	8.4	2.1	9.2	2.0	M	O	Q	3.36	0.48	3.62	0.35	3.48	0.38	238
New York	9.0	2.2	9.3	2.3	9.6	2.1	N	O	Q	3.35	0.45	3.58	0.32	3.46	0.36	2,702
North Carolina	9.1	2.2	8.8	2.3	9.2	2.3	N	O	Q	3.33	0.47	3.55	0.34	3.43	0.38	962
North Dakota	9.0	1.7	8.8	1.8	9.3	1.7	M	O	Q	3.51	0.37	3.73	0.28	3.61	0.30	134
Ohio	9.0	2.0	9.0	2.1	9.4	1.9	N	O	Q	3.41	0.44	3.66	0.31	3.52	0.35	1,485
Oklahoma	8.6	2.1	8.2	2.1	8.7	1.9	M	O	P	3.44	0.42	3.69	0.29	3.55	0.32	383
Oregon	9.5	2.1	9.6	2.2	10.1	1.8	N	O	Q	3.44	0.43	3.63	0.30	3.53	0.34	380
Pennsylvania	9.2	2.0	9.3	2.2	9.7	1.9	N	P	Q	3.40	0.42	3.63	0.31	3.50	0.34	1,423

	MCAT VR		MCAT PS		MCAT BS		MCAT WS			GPA science		GPA non-science		GPA total		Total
	Mean	SD	Mean	SD	Mean	SD	25th%ile	Median	75th	Mean	SD	Mean	SD	Mean	SD	
Puerto Rico	5.9	2.2	6.3	1.7	6.7	2.2	K	L	M	3.21	0.56	3.61	0.35	3.39	0.43	374
Rhode Island	9.2	2.3	9.1	2.4	9.6	2.2	O	P	Q	3.34	0.43	3.60	0.31	3.46	0.36	80
South Carolina	8.8	2.1	8.2	2.1	8.8	2.0	M	O	Q	3.39	0.45	3.56	0.34	3.48	0.37	503
South Dakota	9.1	1.8	8.7	2.2	9.3	2.0	M	O	Q	3.61	0.42	3.70	0.32	3.60	0.36	142
Tennessee	8.6	2.1	8.3	2.2	8.8	2.1	M	O	Q	3.33	0.50	3.61	0.34	3.46	0.39	682
Texas	8.9	2.2	9.1	2.3	9.5	2.1	N	P	Q	3.41	0.44	3.63	0.33	3.47	0.37	3,279
Utah	9.2	1.7	9.3	1.9	10.0	1.7	M	O	Q	3.46	0.38	3.69	0.28	3.56	0.30	486
Vermont	9.6	1.9	9.5	2.1	10.0	1.8	O	P	Q	3.41	0.47	3.56	0.28	3.47	0.31	87
Virginia	9.2	2.1	9.1	2.3	9.5	2.1	N	P	Q	3.31	0.45	3.54	0.34	3.41	0.37	913
Washington	9.5	1.9	9.8	2.0	10.2	1.8	N	P	Q	3.44	0.37	3.65	0.27	3.53	0.30	694
West Virginia	8.7	2.0	8.2	2.1	8.6	2.0	M	O	P	3.40	0.39	3.70	0.27	3.54	0.30	241
Wisconsin	9.4	1.9	9.4	2.1	9.9	1.8	N	O	Q	3.49	0.40	3.68	0.28	3.57	0.32	680
Wyoming	9.1	2.0	8.5	2.0	9.3	1.8	N	O	Q	3.47	0.36	3.66	0.25	3.56	0.28	56
Other U.S. Territories	7.2	1.7	6.6	1.7	7.8	2.1	N	N	P	3.22	0.48	3.64	0.25	3.41	0.36	14
Canada	8.2	2.0	9.6	1.9	10.0	1.9	O	Q	Q	3.38	0.51	3.57	0.36	3.47	0.41	470
Other	8.8	2.2	10.1	2.3	10.2	2.2	N	P	Q	3.45	0.48	3.60	0.34	3.52	0.39	734
All	9.0	2.2	9.1	2.2	9.5	2.1	N	O	Q	3.38	0.45	3.61	0.32	3.48	0.36	39,108

Source: AAMC: Data Warehouse: Applicant Matriculant File as of 10/27/2006.

*** State of Legal Residence not necessarily based on citizenship.

MCAT Scores and GPAs for Matriculants by State of Legal Residence, 2006

Matriculants 2006	MCAT VR		MCAT PS		MCAT BS		MCAT WS			GPA science		GPA non-science		GPA total		Total
	Mean	SD	Mean	SD	Mean	SD	25th%ile	Median	75th	Mean	SD	Mean	SD	Mean	SD	
U.S. State of Legal Residence***																
Alabama	9.8	1.6	9.6	1.9	10.1	1.6	M	O	Q	3.59	0.36	3.77	0.24	3.67	0.28	282
Alaska	9.9	1.9	10.2	1.3	10.6	1.4	N	P	Q	3.56	0.36	3.72	0.25	3.62	0.30	29
Arizona	9.6	1.8	9.6	1.9	10.2	1.7	O	P	Q	3.52	0.38	3.72	0.29	3.62	0.31	223
Arkansas	9.5	1.7	8.9	1.7	9.6	1.3	M	O	P	3.57	0.38	3.75	0.26	3.66	0.29	149
California	9.9	1.7	10.8	1.8	11.0	1.6	O	O	R	3.55	0.33	3.68	0.24	3.60	0.26	1,968
Colorado	10.3	1.5	10.2	1.6	10.7	1.4	O	P	Q	3.59	0.33	3.71	0.26	3.64	0.27	257
Connecticut	10.1	1.6	10.3	1.8	10.7	1.4	O	O	R	3.53	0.32	3.68	0.24	3.60	0.25	195
Delaware	9.6	1.6	10.1	2.0	10.7	1.6	N	P	Q	3.58	0.32	3.72	0.27	3.65	0.28	38
District of Columbia	10.1	2.2	9.9	2.2	10.3	1.7	O	Q	Q	3.48	0.36	3.68	0.25	3.58	0.29	32
Florida	9.6	1.8	9.7	1.8	10.1	1.6	N	O	Q	3.59	0.34	3.76	0.24	3.67	0.27	724
Georgia	9.7	1.6	9.6	2.0	10.1	1.7	N	P	Q	3.51	0.36	3.69	0.26	3.60	0.28	482
Hawaii	9.1	1.7	9.7	2.1	10.2	1.6	O	Q	Q	3.57	0.35	3.70	0.25	3.64	0.27	93
Idaho	10.0	1.6	10.2	1.8	10.5	1.4	N	P	Q	3.86	0.26	3.79	0.19	3.73	0.20	61
Illinois	9.8	1.7	10.0	1.8	10.3	1.6	O	Q	Q	3.52	0.37	3.69	0.28	3.60	0.30	843
Indiana	10.0	1.5	10.2	1.7	10.4	1.6	N	P	Q	3.65	0.33	3.79	0.22	3.72	0.25	330
Iowa	10.3	1.4	10.4	1.6	10.8	1.4	O	P	Q	3.70	0.25	3.83	0.18	3.76	0.20	137
Kansas	9.6	1.6	9.5	1.7	10.0	1.5	N	Q	Q	3.64	0.34	3.78	0.27	3.70	0.25	215
Kentucky	9.5	1.6	9.5	1.9	10.0	1.5	N	Q	Q	3.56	0.37	3.75	0.28	3.64	0.30	216
Louisiana	9.3	1.6	9.3	1.7	9.8	1.4	N	O	Q	3.56	0.36	3.73	0.27	3.64	0.29	399
Maine	10.3	1.3	10.1	1.6	10.4	1.2	O	Q	Q	3.57	0.33	3.70	0.19	3.63	0.24	39
Maryland	10.0	1.7	10.2	1.9	10.7	1.6	O	P	Q	3.54	0.35	3.69	0.26	3.61	0.28	413
Massachusetts	10.2	1.7	10.6	1.9	10.9	1.5	O	O	R	3.55	0.30	3.65	0.25	3.59	0.24	433
Michigan	9.7	1.7	10.3	2.0	10.6	1.7	N	Q	Q	3.56	0.37	3.71	0.27	3.62	0.30	606
Minnesota	10.0	1.6	10.2	1.7	10.6	1.5	O	P	Q	3.63	0.31	3.75	0.22	3.69	0.24	325
Mississippi	9.4	1.6	8.7	1.9	9.6	1.7	M	O	P	3.61	0.42	3.76	0.31	3.68	0.34	138
Missouri	10.1	1.6	10.1	1.8	10.5	1.6	O	P	Q	3.67	0.29	3.77	0.24	3.72	0.25	282

	MCAT VR		MCAT PS		MCAT BS		MCAT WS			GPA science		GPA non-science		GPA total		Total
	Mean	SD	Mean	SD	Mean	SD	25th%ile	Median	75th	Mean	SD	Mean	SD	Mean	SD	
Montana	9.7	1.7	9.7	1.7	10.8	1.3	N	P	Q	3.67	0.26	3.76	0.26	3.71	0.22	50
Nebraska	9.5	1.7	9.4	1.8	9.9	1.7	N	O	Q	3.64	0.32	3.78	0.24	3.70	0.28	129
Nevada	9.4	1.7	9.6	1.8	10.2	1.6	N	O	Q	3.51	0.38	3.76	0.26	3.62	0.28	66
New Hampshire	10.7	1.5	10.4	1.7	11.0	1.4	O	Q	Q	3.63	0.28	3.70	0.21	3.67	0.21	44
New Jersey	9.9	1.6	10.5	1.7	10.8	1.6	O	P	Q	3.59	0.31	3.69	0.24	3.64	0.26	665
New Mexico	9.8	1.8	9.3	2.0	10.1	1.7	N	P	Q	3.55	0.34	3.72	0.28	3.63	0.27	109
New York	9.9	1.7	10.4	1.8	10.7	1.6	O	P	Q	3.55	0.33	3.67	0.26	3.61	0.27	1,317
North Carolina	10.0	1.7	10.0	2.0	10.3	1.7	N	P	Q	3.53	0.35	3.66	0.29	3.59	0.29	394
North Dakota	9.6	1.3	9.2	1.5	10.0	1.4	M	O	Q	3.60	0.31	3.80	0.23	3.69	0.26	54
Ohio	9.6	1.5	10.0	1.8	10.4	1.6	N	P	Q	3.60	0.31	3.76	0.23	3.67	0.25	712
Oklahoma	9.7	1.6	9.2	1.9	9.7	1.8	M	O	Q	3.59	0.34	3.75	0.28	3.66	0.28	182
Oregon	10.2	1.4	10.4	1.8	10.8	1.3	O	P	R	3.62	0.29	3.74	0.22	3.68	0.24	185
Pennsylvania	10.0	1.6	10.4	1.7	10.7	1.4	N	P	Q	3.58	0.33	3.72	0.25	3.64	0.27	675
Puerto Rico	6.9	1.9	7.1	1.5	7.9	1.7	L	M	N	3.42	0.43	3.69	0.27	3.55	0.33	198
Rhode Island	10.3	1.6	10.2	1.6	11.0	1.6	O	Q	R	3.48	0.37	3.67	0.27	3.57	0.28	39
South Carolina	9.6	1.7	9.1	1.9	9.8	1.4	N	O	Q	3.55	0.38	3.69	0.28	3.61	0.31	239
South Dakota	9.7	1.2	9.6	1.9	10.3	1.5	M	P	Q	3.63	0.39	3.76	0.28	3.69	0.32	72
Tennessee	9.5	1.6	9.4	1.9	9.9	1.5	N	O	Q	3.56	0.37	3.71	0.27	3.63	0.30	294
Texas	9.8	1.8	10.2	1.9	10.5	1.6	O	P	Q	3.61	0.32	3.75	0.24	3.68	0.26	1,334
Utah	9.9	1.4	10.3	1.7	10.8	1.4	N	P	Q	3.63	0.26	3.78	0.21	3.70	0.21	224
Vermont	10.4	1.4	10.1	2.0	10.7	1.6	P	P	Q	3.55	0.33	3.60	0.28	3.56	0.26	46
Virginia	10.0	1.7	10.2	1.9	10.7	1.7	O	P	Q	3.49	0.35	3.63	0.30	3.55	0.30	436
Washington	10.1	1.6	10.6	1.7	11.0	1.5	O	Q	R	3.58	0.27	3.72	0.23	3.64	0.25	298
West Virginia	9.4	1.7	9.1	1.8	9.4	1.6	M	O	Q	3.56	0.32	3.76	0.23	3.65	0.28	141
Wisconsin	10.0	1.5	10.3	1.7	10.7	1.4	N	P	Q	3.65	0.29	3.77	0.19	3.71	0.23	317
Wyoming	9.8	1.8	9.4	2.2	10.2	1.8	O	Q	R	3.55	0.32	3.69	0.21	3.60	0.24	24
Other U.S. Territories	8.3	1.3	8.3	1.0	9.3	0.5	O	Q	R	3.50	0.36	3.73	0.14	3.62	0.28	9
Canada	9.0	1.5	11.2	2.0	11.4	1.5	P	Q	Q	3.32	0.32	3.71	0.25	3.70	0.24	30
Other	9.4	1.8	11.0	2.0	11.0	1.8	O	Q	R	3.66	0.27	3.73	0.25	3.70	0.24	187
All	9.8	1.7	10.1	1.9	10.5	1.6	N	P	Q	3.57	0.34	3.71	0.26	3.64	0.27	17,370

Source: AAMC: Data Warehouse: Applicant Matriculant File as of 10/27/2006.

*** State of Legal Residence not necessarily based on citizenship.

MCAT and GPAs for Applicants and Matriculants by Primary Undergraduate Major, 2006

Applicants 2006	MCAT VR		MCAT PS		MCAT BS		MCAT WS			GPA science		GPA non-science		GPA total		Total
	Mean	SD	Mean	SD	Mean	SD	25th%ile	Median	75th	Mean	SD	Mean	SD	Mean	SD	
Biological Sciences	8.8	2.2	8.9	2.2	9.5	2.1	N	O	Q	3.39	0.44	3.64	0.31	3.49	0.36	21,603
Humanities	9.9	1.9	9.2	2.1	9.6	2.0	O	Q	R	3.34	0.48	3.59	0.31	3.48	0.34	1,411
Math and Statistics	9.3	2.2	9.8	2.2	9.5	2.2	N	O	Q	3.42	0.42	3.55	0.35	3.47	0.36	272
Other	9.0	2.2	9.1	2.2	9.5	2.1	N	O	Q	3.37	0.46	3.61	0.32	3.47	0.36	5,741
Physical Sciences	9.2	2.1	10.2	2.2	9.8	2.1	N	O	Q	3.45	0.42	3.57	0.35	3.50	0.36	4,671
Social Sciences	9.2	2.0	8.9	2.1	9.2	2.1	N	P	Q	3.29	0.49	3.54	0.34	3.43	0.37	4,319
Specialized Health Sciences	8.2	2.3	8.0	2.2	8.5	2.2	M	O	P	3.34	0.47	3.59	0.34	3.46	0.37	1,091
All	9.0	2.2	9.1	2.2	9.5	2.1	N	O	Q	3.38	0.45	3.61	0.32	3.48	0.36	39,108

Matriculants 2006	MCAT VR	MCAT PS	MCAT BS	MCAT WS		GPA	GPA non-	GPA total	Total

	Mean	SD	Mean	SD	Mean	SD	25th%ile	Median	75th	science Mean	SD	science Mean	SD	Mean	SD	
Biological Sciences	9.7	1.7	9.9	1.9	10.5	1.6	N	P	Q	3.59	0.33	3.74	0.24	3.65	0.27	9,439
Humanities	10.5	1.5	10.1	1.6	10.4	1.5	O	Q	R	3.52	0.35	3.67	0.25	3.61	0.25	750
Math and Statistics	10.1	1.7	10.9	1.7	10.5	1.5	O	P	Q	3.62	0.30	3.65	0.31	3.63	0.28	130
Other	9.8	1.7	10.1	1.9	10.4	1.6	N	P	Q	3.56	0.34	3.71	0.24	3.65	0.26	2,387
Physical Sciences	9.9	1.7	11.0	1.8	10.7	1.6	N	P	Q	3.61	0.32	3.67	0.28	3.63	0.26	2,328
Social Sciences	10.1	1.6	9.9	1.8	10.2	1.6	O	P	Q	3.50	0.36	3.65	0.26	3.58	0.28	1,960
Specialized Health Sciences	9.4	1.6	9.4	1.9	9.9	1.6	N	O	Q	3.54	0.35	3.72	0.24	3.63	0.27	376
All	9.8	1.7	10.1	1.9	10.5	1.6	N	P	Q	3.57	0.34	3.71	0.26	3.64	0.27	17,370

Source: AAMC: Data Warehouse: Applicant Matriculant File as of 10/27/2006.

Applicant Age at Anticipated Matriculation, 2003-2006

Applicant Age at Anticipated Matriculation 2003 on			2003 Matriculated N Mean	Y Mean	All Mean	2004 Matriculated N Mean	Y Mean	All Mean	2005 Matriculated N Mean	Y Mean	All Mean	2006 Matriculated N Mean	Y Mean	All Mean
Women	Hispanic	Mexican American	25	24	25	25	24	25	25	24	24	25	24	24
		Puerto Rican	23	23	23	24	23	23	24	23	23	24	23	23
		Cuban	25	23	24	24	23	23	24	23	23	23	23	23
		Other Hispanic	25	24	24	25	23	24	25	23	24	25	24	24
		Multiple Hispanic	24	24	24	25	24	25	24	24	24	24	24	24
		Subtotal	24	24	24	25	23	24	25	23	24	24	24	24
	Non-Hispanic	Black	25	24	25	25	24	25	25	24	25	25	24	25
		Asian	24	23	23	24	23	23	24	23	23	24	23	23
		Native American (incl AK)	25	24	25	28	25	26	27	24	26	25	25	25
		Native Hawaiian/OPI	24	22	23	24	23	24	24	24	25	25	25	25
		White	25	23	24	24	23	24	24	24	24	24	23	24
		Other	24	23	24	26	23	25	25	26	25	25	23	24
		Unknown	24	22	23	25	22	23	24	21	22	24	22	22
		Multiple Race	25	24	24	25	24	24	24	24	24	24	24	24
		Subtotal	25	23	24	24	23	24	24	23	24	24	23	24
	Non-U.S.	Foreign	24	24	24	24	23	24	24	23	24	24	24	24
		Unknown Citizenship							25		25			
		Subtotal	24	24	24	24	23	24	24	23	24	24	24	24
	Total For Women		24	24	24	24	23	24	24	23	24	24	23	24
Men	Hispanic	Mexican American	25	25	25	26	25	25	26	25	25	26	24	25
		Puerto Rican	24	23	23	25	23	23	25	23	24	25	23	24
		Cuban	23	24	24	25	24	24	24	24	23	24	24	24
		Other Hispanic	26	24	25	26	24	25	26	24	25	26	24	25
		Multiple Hispanic	26	24	24	25	24	24	25	25	24	25	24	24
		Subtotal	25	24	25	26	24	25	26	24	25	26	24	25
	Non-Hispanic	Black	27	24	26	27	24	26	27	24	26	26	24	25
		Asian	24	23	24	24	23	24	24	23	24	24	23	24
		Native American (incl AK)	26	25	27	28	26	27	28	26	27	27	25	26
		Native Hawaiian/OPI	24	24	24	25	23	24	25	24	24	25	25	25
		White	25	24	24	25	24	24	25	24	24	25	24	25
		Other	24	23	24	24	25	25	25	25	25	25	24	25
		Unknown	26	23	24	26	22	24	26	22	24	25	22	23
		Multiple Race	25	24	24	25	24	25	25	24	24	25	24	25
		Subtotal	25	24	24	25	24	24	25	24	24	25	24	24

Non-U.S.	Foreign	24	24	24	24	24	24	24	24	24	24	24	24
	Subtotal	24	24	24	24	24	24	24	24	24	24	24	24
	Total for Men	25	24	24	25	24	24	25	24	24	25	24	24
All Applicants	Hispanic	Mexican American	25	25	25	25	24	25	25	24	25	25	24	25
		Puerto Rican	24	23	23	24	23	24	24	23	24	24	23	23
		Cuban	24	24	24	25	23	24	24	23	23	24	23	24
		Other Hispanic	25	24	25	25	24	25	25	24	25	25	24	25
		Multiple Hispanic	25	25	25	25	24	25	25	24	25	24	24	24
		Subtotal	25	24	24	25	24	24	25	24	24	25	24	24
	Non-Hispanic	Black	26	24	25	25	24	25	25	24	25	26	24	25
		Asian	24	23	23	24	23	23	24	23	24	24	23	24
		Native American (incl AK)	27	25	26	28	25	27	27	25	27	26	25	26
		Native Hawaiian/OPI	24	23	24	25	24	25	25	24	25	25	25	25
		White	25	24	24	25	24	24	25	24	24	25	24	24
		Other	24	23	24	25	25	25	25	25	25	25	24	25
		Unknown	25	22	23	25	22	23	25	22	23	24	22	23
		Multiple Race	25	24	24	25	24	24	25	24	24	25	24	24
		Subtotal	25	24	24	25	24	24	25	24	24	25	24	24
	Non-U.S.	Foreign	24	24	24	24	23	24	24	23	24	24	24	24
		Unknown Citizenship								25		25		
		Subtotal	24	24	24	24	23	24	24	23	24	24	24	24
Total for Women and Men			25	24	24	25	24	24	25	24	24	25	24	24

Source: AAMC: Data Warehouse: Applicant Matriculant File as of 10/27/2006.

Applicants by State of Legal Residence and Race and Ethnicity, 2006

2006 Applicants	Hispanic					Non-Hispanic								Non-U.S.	Total
	Mexican American	Puerto Rican	Cuban	Other Hispanic	Multiple Hispanic	Black	Asian	Native American (incl AK)	Native Hawaiian/OPI	White	Other	Unknown	Multiple Race	Foreign	
Northeast Connecticut	2	1	0	10	2	13	68	0		294	1	4	9	9	414
Delaware	0	0	0	2	0	18	14	0		39	0	2	1	2	78
District of Columbia	0	1	0	2	0	26	4	1		35	0	1	2	13	87
Maine	0	1	0	0	0	0	2	1		77	0	1	1	1	84
Maryland	3	5	3	24	5	149	224	0	5	433	2	12	22	21	913
Massachusetts	2	5	1	18	2	45	130	0	0	628	0	12	24	29	897
New Hampshire	0	0	0	1	0	0	7	0	0	82	0	2	4	1	97
New Jersey	1	17	11	44	5	110	479	2	5	624	2	28	19	11	1,358
New York	8	30	9	75	9	299	621	1	6	1,473	1	55	60	55	2,702
Pennsylvania	4	12	1	18	3	81	227	2	2	1,023	0	9	32	11	1,423
Rhode Island	0	0	1	6	0	7	10	0	0	51	0	6	0	1	80
Vermont	1	0	0	2	0	0	2	0	0	76	0	2	3	1	87
Central Illinois	37	8	5	29	6	168	534	0	5	1,002	2	11	27	12	1,844
Indiana	8	3	1	6	2	31	86	2	0	540	0	8	8	8	702
Iowa	2	0	0	2	0	7	35	0	0	286	0	4	4	1	341
Kansas	9	1	0	3	0	16	58	3	1	312	0	10	11	5	434
Michigan	19	4	2	15	2	106	256	0	0	869	1	14	35	19	1,347
Minnesota	3	3	1	3	0	10	69	5	0	625	0		28	9	761
Missouri	7	2	0	14	0	30	64	1	0	375	0	63	7	5	568

	Nebraska	3	0	0	2	0	9	20	0	0	249	0	2	5	1	291
	North Dakota	1	0	0	0	0	0	6	1	0	125	0	0	0	1	134
	Ohio	8	6	2	20	2	82	255	2	0	1,054	1	15	22	16	1,485
	South Dakota	0	0	0	0	0	1	5	2	0	133	0	0	1	0	142
	Wisconsin	5	0	0	7	0	17	58	2	0	567	0	6	15	5	680
South	Alabama	2	2	1	5	0	64	66	2	1	361	0	2	10	6	542
	Arkansas	5	0	0	6	0	25	26	2	0	229	0	1	8	3	305
	Florida	20	35	122	141	18	209	273	5	6	841	2	19	40	17	1,748
	Georgia	4	8	4	27	4	240	186	2	0	623	2	3	29	22	1,154
	Kentucky	0	0	1	2	0	10	44	0	0	329	0	5	13	8	412
	Louisiana	11	3	6	27	1	107	89	2	3	623	0	2	10	2	886
	Mississippi	0	1	0	4	0	63	25	1	0	214	0	1	4	1	314
	North Carolina	8	5	3	14	0	103	144	8	2	634	0	5	23	13	962
	Oklahoma	2	1	0	4	0	19	52	34	1	242	1	3	19	5	383
	Puerto Rico	1	347	0	3	8	1	1	0	0	2	0	3	2	0	374
	South Carolina	3	1	1	6	0	72	42	1	1	359	0	3	12	2	503
	Tennessee	3	4	0	4	0	92	63	3	0	484	0	4	13	12	682
	Texas	356	17	3	113	3	275	820	20	4	1,524	52	5	43	37	3,276
	Virginia	8	7	1	24	3	99	171	1	2	544	2	11	29	11	913
	West Virginia	2	0	0	3	0	2	28	0	0	199	0	0	6	1	241
	U.S. Territories and Possessions	0	0	0	2	0	6	0	0	3	1	0	0	2	0	14
West	Alaska	2	0	0	2	0	3	3	3	0	67	0	0	5	0	85
	Arizona	46	3	2	15	1	19	77	10	2	382	0	4	11	2	574
	California	253	17	12	147	22	194	1,716	8	35	1,740	11	67	174	56	4,452
	Colorado	29	1	0	12	2	14	47	4	1	505	1	6	20	4	646
	Hawaii	0	4	0	12	0	1	121	0	13	20	0	1	42	0	214
	Idaho	1	0	0	1	0	1	6	1	0	140	0	0	0	0	150
	Montana	0	0	0	0	0	0	3	4	1	90	0	0	3	0	101
	Nevada	7	1	2	6	0	4	33	1	1	102	0	2	5	1	165
	New Mexico	47	0	0	22	5	3	17	3	1	133	0	1	6	1	238
	Oregon	6	1	0	8	0	7	46	2	1	289	1	3	13		380
	Utah	5	2	1	7	0	2	19	2	3	432	1	2	9	3	488
	Washington	9	0	2	13	2	11	145	0	2	460	1	6	29	5	694
	Wyoming	0	0	0	0	0	0	2	0	0	52	0	1	1	0	56
Non-US	Foreign	0	0	0	2	0	2	19	0	0	25	0	2	2	1,074	1,126
	Unknown	2	1	0	5	1	11	16	0	0	37	0	1	2	1	78
Total		955	560	206	935	115	2,906	7,532	145	111	22,669	84	437	925	1,527	39,108

Source: AAMC: Data Warehouse: Applicant Matriculant File as of 10/27/2006.

Total Enrollment by Sex and School, 2002-2006

Total Active Enrollment as of October 31		2002			2003			2004			2005			2006		
State	School	Female	Male	All	Female	Male	All	Female	Male	All	Female	Male	All	Female	Male	All
AL	Alabama	269	369	638	268	375	643	269	378	647	265	371	636	268	385	653
	South Alabama	118	135	253	115	135	250	116	140	256	128	135	263	140	136	276
AR	Arkansas	203	331	534	216	331	547	226	326	552	246	333	579	263	336	599
AZ	Arizona	199	209	408	212	208	420	210	206	416	224	224	448	235	225	460
CA	Loma Linda	278	368	646	303	348	651	311	360	671	314	364	678	318	387	705
	Southern Cal - Keck	288	374	662	304	346	650	313	342	655	325	332	657	331	333	664
	Stanford	232	217	449	235	222	457	234	220	454	226	232	458	214	229	443
	UC Berkeley/SF Joint Prog	27	9	36	26	10	36	23	13	36	19	17	36	18	17	35

	UC Davis	210	180	390	206	178	384	214	176	390	205	171	376	206	165	371
	UC Irvine	174	206	380	178	194	372	178	191	369	183	196	379	197	211	408
	UC San Diego	237	273	510	244	263	507	249	258	507	237	254	491	243	251	494
	UC San Francisco	338	282	620	348	273	621	333	265	598	339	261	600	342	261	603
	UCLA - Geffen	306	290	596	299	308	607	304	286	590	305	286	591	304	304	608
	UCLA Drew	50	42	92	51	46	97	58	36	94	66	33	99	64	40	104
CO	Colorado	253	267	520	241	272	513	257	280	537	264	283	547	277	295	572
CT	Connecticut	175	135	310	179	129	308	190	129	319	200	119	319	206	122	328
	Yale	227	257	484	249	238	487	255	233	488	247	212	459	240	219	459
DC	George Washington	335	308	643	362	293	655	382	282	664	382	296	678	391	304	695
	Georgetown	330	342	672	343	341	684	348	325	673	361	344	705	390	368	758
	Howard	220	214	434	238	193	431	260	209	469	237	209	446	249	230	479
FL	Florida	229	218	447	228	225	453	234	228	462	258	232	490	256	245	501
	Florida State	21	44	65	40	71	111	70	99	169	108	112	220	172	120	292
	Miami-Miller	307	265	572	294	277	571	302	284	586	313	325	638	311	340	651
	South Florida	190	206	396	194	218	412	220	219	439	245	211	456	251	226	477
GA	Emory	216	233	449	225	229	454	223	242	465	233	236	469	235	230	465
	Georgia	279	435	714	295	417	712	313	396	709	312	400	712	333	411	744
	Mercer	97	119	216	98	123	221	115	118	233	117	125	242	119	126	245
	Morehouse	108	53	161	112	66	178	124	66	190	125	71	196	126	84	210
HI	Hawaii - Burns	115	128	243	132	123	255	147	99	246	151	106	257	144	111	255
IA	Iowa - Carver	257	334	591	267	316	583	270	310	580	266	298	563	282	291	573
IL	Chicago - Pritzker	207	190	397	224	212	436	227	218	445	228	226	454	232	240	472
	Chicago Med-Rosalind Franklin	285	460	745	292	453	745	319	442	761	343	410	753	328	423	751
	Illinois	538	727	1,265	594	735	1,329	621	690	1,311	640	675	1,315	662	681	1,343
	Loyola - Stritch	245	274	519	253	278	531	266	275	541	275	276	551	279	283	562
	Northwestern - Feinberg	315	381	696	324	370	694	318	376	694	328	350	678	351	358	709
	Rush	249	232	481	261	234	495	284	227	511	280	231	511	289	239	528
	Southern Illinois	137	144	281	154	140	294	153	138	291	153	140	293	155	137	292
IN	Indiana	479	626	1,105	504	618	1,122	525	614	1,139	525	629	1,154	509	650	1,159
KS	Kansas	313	371	684	313	380	693	317	386	703	309	390	699	306	384	690
KY	Kentucky	159	209	368	166	214	380	168	228	396	171	231	402	164	241	405
	Louisville	286	284	570	295	297	592	279	295	574	255	328	583	242	353	595
LA	LSU New Orleans	311	373	684	328	372	700	336	357	693	323	369	692	304	375	679
	LSU Shreveport	172	231	403	168	237	405	176	229	405	175	233	408	185	242	427
	Tulane	263	351	614	244	326	570	265	360	625	279	336	615	272	349	621
MA	Boston	258	341	599	280	315	595	305	313	623	332	301	633	359	305	664
	Harvard	341	361	702	349	340	689	355	359	714	368	365	733	385	376	761
	Massachusetts	202	199	401	221	204	425	225	194	419	225	186	411	233	190	423
	Tufts	324	373	697	333	356	689	327	364	691	316	375	691	315	375	690
MD	Johns Hopkins	214	260	474	229	241	470	233	247	480	235	230	465	231	253	484
	Maryland	330	259	589	337	254	591	359	246	605	364	244	608	370	244	614
	Uniformed Services-Hebert	168	484	652	195	466	661	208	449	657	206	462	668	206	473	679
MI	Michigan	294	375	669	298	376	674	292	391	683	310	377	687	323	365	688
	Michigan State	254	184	438	249	177	426	247	184	431	253	195	448	252	203	455
	Wayne State	463	548	1,011	474	551	1,025	492	558	1,050	508	557	1,065	532	559	1,091
MN	Mayo	89	76	165	79	85	164	81	84	165	84	82	166	84	78	162
	Minnesota Duluth	48	60	108	53	58	111	49	60	109	52	53	105	56	56	112
	Minnesota Twin Cities	369	391	760	384	398	782	399	401	800	403	394	797	361	375	736
MO	Missouri Columbia	180	192	372	178	195	371	175	193	368	178	189	367	183	187	370
	Missouri	308	164	372	310	153	463	300	144	353	214	151	366	208	161	370

State	Institution															
	Kansas City															
	St Louis	280	323	603	281	340	621	277	330	607	265	349	614	272	371	643
	Washington U St Louis	230	232	462	223	244	467	229	235	464	238	236	474	224	214	436
MS	Mississippi	151	245	396	150	245	365	164	242	406	163	239	402	181	232	413
NC	Duke	202	240	442	210	238	448	217	230	447	221	240	461	224	232	456
	East Carolina - Brody	139	155	294	145	157	302	146	146	292	140	145	285	140	146	286
	North Carolina	320	313	633	338	305	643	330	319	649	322	317	639	317	326	643
	Wake Forest	173	254	427	173	263	436	181	244	425	189	241	430	191	252	443
ND	North Dakota	109	112	221	116	111	227	121	109	230	121	112	233	121	121	242
NE	Creighton	215	244	459	216	240	456	227	236	463	225	256	481	235	263	498
	Nebraska	186	280	466	178	281	459	197	278	475	198	281	479	209	272	481
NH	Dartmouth	121	136	257	135	146	281	151	152	303	146	157	303	149	168	317
NJ	UMDNJ - RW Johnson	310	347	657	314	321	635	326	295	621	341	292	633	346	301	647
	UMDNJ New Jersey	303	379	682	313	360	673	328	357	685	335	349	684	333	355	688
NM	New Mexico	171	131	302	175	126	301	181	108	289	175	125	300	167	137	304
NV	Nevada	88	118	206	101	109	210	104	110	214	105	107	212	111	106	217
NY	Albany	256	252	508	253	249	502	270	250	520	293	245	538	298	242	540
	Buffalo	297	265	562	297	265	562	290	265	555	309	247	556	293	259	552
	Columbia	286	359	645	281	323	604	282	313	595	293	325	618	290	319	609
	Cornell - Weill	197	206	403	201	205	406	191	193	384	203	193	396	196	194	390
	Einstein	318	324	642	326	336	662	347	345	692	365	330	695	407	355	762
	Mount Sinai	232	220	452	255	218	473	262	226	488	246	225	471	255	223	478
	New York Medical	383	380	763	392	365	757	380	376	756	384	379	763	396	378	774
	New York University	319	365	684	346	362	708	344	355	699	349	354	703	354	357	711
	Rochester	204	173	377	217	181	398	220	181	401	213	176	389	205	176	381
	SUNY Downstate	387	393	780	385	383	768	389	388	777	372	392	764	376	377	753
	SUNY Upstate	267	360	627	283	335	618	286	318	604	291	315	606	309	301	610
	Stony Brook	225	207	432	226	202	428	240	206	446	233	210	443	225	211	436
OH	Case Western	234	331	565	249	329	578	256	350	606	281	341	622	301	369	670
	Cincinnati	241	369	610	246	371	617	253	366	619	275	352	627	268	348	616
	Northeastern Ohio	225	200	426	213	205	418	228	198	426	233	229	462	240	221	461
	Ohio State	358	475	833	367	479	846	345	502	847	312	525	837	322	511	833
	Toledo	230	346	576	232	356	588	246	345	591	239	361	600	253	354	607
	Wright State - Boonshoft	198	157	355	154	125	279	212	159	371	209	175	384	226	172	398
OK	Oklahoma	222	353	575	234	339	573	227	344	571	224	352	576	239	368	607
OR	Oregon	200	189	389	231	187	418	252	190	442	244	194	438	267	210	477
PA	Drexel	514	486	1,000	495	519	1,014	496	497	995	503	503	1,006	510	506	1,016
	Jefferson	405	493	898	435	493	928	457	466	923	457	471	928	491	466	957
	Penn State	248	220	468	272	223	495	281	229	510	287	236	523	279	271	550
	Pennsylvania	319	407	726	255	319	574	339	376	715	354	370	724	351	364	715
	Pittsburgh	273	294	567	285	300	585	274	299	573	268	311	579	275	316	591
	Temple	347	467	814	363	426	789	348	406	754	342	398	740	332	387	719
PR	Caribe	107	121	228	113	118	231	130	126	256	137	122	259	130	127	257
	Ponce	105	140	245	103	137	240	119	144	263	120	141	261	127	135	262
	Puerto Rico	249	197	446	251	200	451	246	201	447	241	220	461	237	233	470
RI	Brown	183	138	321	192	134	326	184	138	322	195	145	340	201	155	356
SC	MU South Carolina	255	308	563	274	308	582	268	302	570	279	293	572	277	307	584
	South Carolina	130	161	291	138	156	294	147	157	304	154	163	317	142	168	310
SD	South Dakota	84	122	206	86	116	202	91	112	203	98	107	205	96	109	205
TN	East Tennessee - Quillen	117	114	231	114	111	225	115	118	233	118	119	237	107	127	234
	Meharry	188	164	352	176	178	354	187	172	359	189	178	367	215	173	388
	Tennessee	256	383	639	257	366	623	243	366	609	228	377	605	234	371	605
	Vanderbilt	164	241	405	192	228	420	196	232	428	200	238	438	193	234	427

State	School	Female	Male	All	Female	Male	All	Female	Male	All	Female	Male	All	Female	Male	All
TX	Baylor	342	327	669	347	336	682	331	336	667	326	353	679	316	356	672
	Texas A & M	143	132	275	144	130	274	146	143	289	154	147	301	172	154	326
	Texas Tech	187	303	490	197	297	494	213	312	525	231	301	532	244	309	553
	UT Galveston	343	448	791	383	431	814	400	405	805	404	412	816	429	434	863
	UT Houston	376	437	813	387	428	815	394	438	832	409	445	854	402	472	874
	UT San Antonio	422	390	812	432	382	814	457	361	818	476	350	826	496	356	852
	UT Southwestern	336	489	825	370	479	849	378	497	875	390	512	902	412	505	917
UT	Utah	150	254	404	159	250	409	155	259	414	156	256	412	154	253	407
VA	Eastern Virginia	206	205	411	223	201	424	224	198	422	235	204	439	226	221	447
	Virginia	270	273	543	263	284	547	272	274	546	284	276	560	258	294	552
	Virginia Commonwealth	342	352	694	355	358	713	347	369	716	354	380	734	353	371	724
VT	Vermont	219	157	376	233	157	390	250	154	404	252	162	414	253	171	424
WA	U Washington	399	362	761	406	372	778	414	363	777	423	380	803	405	385	790
WI	MC Wisconsin	318	487	805	333	459	792	355	449	804	356	453	809	382	424	806
	Wisconsin	307	257	564	305	264	569	330	277	607	330	287	617	325	297	622
WV	Marshall - Edwards	84	106	190	86	104	190	81	104	185	82	124	206	90	133	223
	West Virginia	143	218	361	147	222	369	169	223	392	168	251	419	161	259	420
All		30,797	35,049	65,846	31,716	34,588	66,304	32,696	34,507	67,203	33,184	34,824	68,008	33,736	35,431	69,167

Source: AAMC: Data Warehouse: STUDENT file, as of 11/9/2006.

Total Graduates by School and Sex, 2002-2006

	Graduates	Class of 2002			Class of 2003			Class of 2004			Class of 2005			Class of 2006		
State	School	Female	Male	All	Female	Male	All	Female	Male	All	Female	Male	All	Female	Male	All
AL	Alabama	58	97	155	68	89	157	63	97	160	74	92	166	63	102	165
	South Alabama	25	35	60	36	23	59	23	37	60	24	35	59	25	35	60
AR	Arkansas	46	93	139	44	86	130	52	82	134	51	77	128	47	84	131
AZ	Arizona	49	52	101	43	51	94	48	55	103	46	45	91	43	46	89
CA	Loma Linda	57	97	154	58	89	147	66	79	145	68	63	131	60	83	143
	Southern Cal-Keck	69	85	154	62	109	171	80	80	160	64	96	160	77	84	161
	Stanford	51	35	86	50	42	92	40	50	90	44	25	69	58	40	98
	UC Davis	41	51	92	50	43	93	45	41	86	46	56	102	55	37	92
	UC Irvine	43	50	93	37	55	92	50	46	96	38	49	87	40	40	80
	UC San Diego	41	56	97	66	76	142	48	60	108	58	66	124	53	64	117
	UC San Francisco	78	57	135	88	67	155	89	74	163	77	73	150	84	58	142
	UCLA-Geffen	56	69	125	75	67	142	72	82	154	80	69	149	70	62	132
	UCLA/DrewJoint Program	14	12	26	12	5	17	11	11	22	13	9	22	14	7	21
CO	Colorado	66	60	126	67	66	133	48	65	113	64	64	128	59	65	124
CT	Connecticut	34	43	77	44	36	80	39	29	68	39	34	73	41	35	76
	Yale	55	57	112	36	61	97	52	57	109	46	49	95	57	44	101
DC	George Washington	82	67	149	68	85	153	68	82	150	97	56	153	88	68	156
	Georgetown	81	82	163	79	85	163	84	94	178	71	85	156	79	71	150
	Howard	40	55	95	40	42	82	47	38	85	62	43	105	53	42	95
FL	Florida	57	50	107	53	57	110	60	56	116	49	50	99	65	50	115
	Florida State	0	0	0	0	0	0	0	0	0	11	16	27	9	27	36
	Miami-Miller	78	70	148	72	62	134	70	72	142	71	57	128	80	72	152

	South Florida	42	62	104	46	50	96	41	49	90	39	64	103	56	37	93
GA	Emory	36	67	103	53	58	111	55	51	106	43	60	103	56	54	110
	Georgia	54	118	172	64	116	180	55	118	173	72	96	168	71	85	156
	Mercer	23	25	48	23	29	52	17	25	42	23	31	54	25	29	54
	Morehouse	22	13	35	24	11	35	22	17	39	28	16	44	30	8	38
HI	Hawaii-Burns	22	31	53	22	31	53	26	40	66	27	29	56	39	25	64
IA	Iowa-Carver	66	97	163	60	87	147	60	71	131	64	87	151	65	70	135
IL	Chicago Med-Rosalind Franklin	69	117	186	58	111	169	61	107	168	71	121	192	80	97	177
	Chicago-Pritzker	57	54	111	48	42	90	52	50	102	48	54	102	57	48	105
	Illinois	116	164	280	110	171	281	126	181	307	122	170	292	120	148	268
	Loyola-Stritch	54	69	123	59	70	129	62	72	134	61	67	128	67	64	131
	Northwestern-Feinberg	74	94	168	81	83	164	82	91	173	68	99	167	68	83	151
	Rush	59	61	120	56	49	105	53	55	108	65	58	123	60	63	123
	Southern Illinois	31	36	67	29	40	69	36	36	72	38	29	67	35	37	72
IN	Indiana	106	167	273	106	155	261	106	149	255	115	144	259	128	130	258
KS	Kansas	75	98	173	63	92	155	82	76	158	76	97	173	82	92	174
KY	Kentucky	31	58	89	41	47	88	39	46	85	40	56	96	43	52	95
	Louisville	66	64	130	66	69	135	63	73	136	79	66	145	75	65	140
LA	LSU New Orleans	75	96	171	67	93	160	78	99	177	77	88	165	82	93	175
	LSU Shreveport	38	58	96	43	53	96	40	59	99	47	55	102	37	56	93
	Tulane	62	85	147	64	89	153	74	82	156	58	87	145	67	85	152
MA	Boston	60	88	148	57	98	155	59	80	139	62	76	138	70	84	154
	Harvard	69	88	157	68	97	165	87	90	177	75	72	147	77	75	152
	Massachusetts	46	43	89	51	45	96	50	48	98	52	52	104	43	45	93
	Tufts	68	96	164	77	94	171	76	91	167	85	77	162	78	96	174
MD	Johns Hopkins	54	60	114	47	69	116	54	61	115	46	77	123	49	53	102
	Maryland	65	73	138	76	59	135	67	70	137	77	65	142	87	60	147
	Uniformed Services-Hebert	35	128	163	40	113	153	35	131	166	56	109	165	41	122	163
MI	Michigan	75	88	163	70	84	154	74	92	166	68	95	163	75	94	169
	Michigan State	55	41	96	63	47	110	61	48	109	60	40	100	56	41	97
	Wayne State	111	132	243	102	130	232	108	137	245	108	131	239	113	131	244
MN	Mayo	20	20	40	23	20	43	21	22	43	21	20	41	20	20	40
	Minnesota Twin Cities	95	115	210	99	108	207	102	105	207	94	128	222	123	101	224
MO	Missouri Columbia	40	53	93	41	49	90	43	49	92	48	41	89	38	51	89
	Missouri Kansas City	62	36	98	45	35	80	59	36	95	45	35	80	51	41	92
	St Louis	63	76	139	66	72	138	60	81	141	72	79	151	66	79	145
	Washington U St Louis	58	51	109	57	52	109	58	58	116	52	60	112	59	62	121
MS	Mississippi	29	71	100	42	61	103	37	53	90	33	69	102	35	62	97
NC	Duke	35	50	85	39	47	86	44	59	103	41	42	83	51	58	109
	East Carolina-Brody	37	32	69	29	36	65	39	43	82	37	34	71	34	36	70
	North Carolina	65	86	151	60	74	134	74	79	153	74	80	154	83	63	146
	Wake Forest	36	63	99	39	52	91	42	67	109	38	68	106	44	55	99
ND	North Dakota	27	28	55	28	27	55	20	35	55	28	28	50	33	22	55
NE	Creighton	44	58	102	55	57	112	42	66	108	56	50	106	55	58	113
	Nebraska	55	62	117	50	71	121	37	69	106	47	63	110	42	79	121
NH	Dartmouth	24	22	46	26	34	60	22	27	49	32	37	69	24	32	56
NJ	UMDNJ New Jersey	66	100	166	70	98	168	70	92	162	76	92	168	72	90	162
	UMDNJ-RW Johnson	51	83	134	76	85	161	66	84	150	63	75	138	82	64	146
NM	New Mexico	40	27	67	36	34	70	34	38	72	46	22	68	43	22	65
NV	Nevada	21	25	46	16	32	48	25	25	50	25	28	53	24	30	54
NY	Albany	66	59	125	64	61	125	60	58	118	63	58	121	56	65	131
	Buffalo	62	74	136	75	65	140	81	61	142	65	73	138	76	58	134

State	School															
	Columbia	67	80	147	70	84	154	67	83	150	62	73	135	74	90	164
	Cornell-Weill	53	48	101	51	47	98	56	54	110	44	45	89	49	52	101
	Einstein	80	97	177	84	77	161	82	83	166	83	96	179	70	76	146
	Mount Sinai	53	50	103	52	58	110	53	55	108	61	54	115	57	54	111
	New York Medical	94	102	196	93	97	190	98	89	187	97	96	193	96	89	185
	New York University	68	85	153	76	81	157	75	91	166	74	95	169	81	74	155
	Rochester	52	57	109	39	41	80	56	47	103	55	46	101	54	45	99
	SUNY Downstate	94	100	194	101	96	197	98	93	191	109	93	202	93	107	200
	SUNY Upstate	66	83	149	63	100	163	64	88	152	67	88	155	69	87	156
	Stony Brook	48	65	113	51	56	107	51	55	106	58	54	112	65	52	117
OH	Case Western	62	86	148	47	74	121	58	87	145	56	87	143	55	77	132
	Cincinnati	42	113	155	61	92	153	63	86	149	47	101	148	68	85	153
	MC Ohio	44	88	132	49	81	130	50	84	134	56	73	129	57	83	140
	Northeastern Ohio	44	57	101	52	48	100	50	52	102	55	44	99	57	54	111
	Ohio State	81	127	208	71	118	189	88	114	202	104	107	211	80	122	202
	Wright State	46	48	94	45	33	78	45	41	86	54	32	86	46	40	86
OK	Oklahoma	52	84	136	46	96	142	62	78	140	57	83	140	54	81	135
OR	Oregon	46	47	93	37	49	86	36	50	86	58	51	109	51	48	99
	Drexel	120	102	222	132	101	233	110	112	222	121	112	233	121	124	245
	Jefferson	111	114	225	85	114	199	104	127	231	107	121	228	102	115	217
PA	Penn State	43	59	102	45	52	97	57	58	115	63	58	121	78	47	125
	Pennsylvania	59	69	128	63	85	148	68	88	156	63	86	149	77	81	158
	Pittsburgh	63	73	136	67	56	123	75	76	151	71	71	142	52	74	126
	Temple	61	102	163	69	130	199	89	110	199	82	108	190	97	101	198
	Caribe	21	31	52	27	26	53	27	27	54	23	34	57	28	30	58
PR	Ponce	25	36	61	25	30	55	13	35	48	21	32	53	31	35	66
	Puerto Rico	51	56	107	48	52	100	57	55	112	62	37	99	55	36	91
RI	Brown	42	33	75	41	42	83	52	35	87	40	33	73	50	39	89
SC	MU South Carolina	56	74	130	55	75	130	62	79	141	57	78	135	72	70	142
	South Carolina	29	42	71	26	47	73	28	38	66	31	34	65	43	40	83
SD	South Dakota	21	30	51	20	32	52	18	32	50	17	31	48	27	24	51
	East Tennessee-Quillen	30	29	59	26	36	62	25	25	50	28	26	54	30	28	58
TN	Meharry	42	45	87	55	27	82	32	42	74	42	29	71	33	33	66
	Tennessee	61	97	158	60	100	160	65	89	154	67	80	147	52	94	146
	Vanderbilt	42	62	104	36	57	93	47	60	107	41	49	90	48	63	111
	Baylor	70	90	160	87	81	168	89	82	171	78	77	155	88	82	170
	Texas A & M	38	27	65	38	30	68	30	30	60	35	33	68	29	30	59
	Texas Tech	48	72	120	36	74	110	47	65	112	47	82	129	42	75	117
TX	UT Galveston	98	97	195	76	104	180	77	117	194	99	101	200	86	97	183
	UT Houston	80	135	215	75	111	186	91	101	192	81	103	184	104	98	202
	UT San Antonio	101	89	190	99	95	194	106	94	200	85	109	194	106	87	193
	UT Southwestern	77	124	201	75	114	189	86	118	204	86	125	211	91	126	217
UT	Utah	27	72	99	38	63	99	41	59	100	30	62	92	38	64	102
	Eastern Virginia	47	52	99	43	53	96	53	56	109	46	43	89	59	45	104
VA	Virginia	50	85	135	66	63	129	55	79	134	53	73	126	81	56	137
	Virginia Commonwealth	74	94	168	72	91	163	91	80	171	82	83	165	89	97	186
VT	Vermont	37	56	93	51	43	94	55	35	90	53	35	88	60	37	97
WA	U Washington	88	94	182	77	80	157	90	82	172	82	79	161	103	74	182
WI	MC Wisconsin	67	127	194	77	127	204	67	121	188	83	105	188	76	123	199
	Wisconsin	74	61	135	81	62	143	65	68	133	84	64	148	80	65	145
WV	Marshall-Edwards	19	28	47	23	27	50	20	23	43	20	23	43	21	26	47
	West Virginia	28	46	74	36	51	87	26	51	77	39	42	81	38	61	99
All		6,925	8,755	15,680	7,033	8,507	15,540	7,262	8,568	15,830	7,415	8,349	15,764	7,746	8,179	15,925

Source: AAMC: Data Warehouse: Applicant Matriculant File and SRS tables as of 11/9/2006.

Total Graduates by Race/Ethnicity within Sex, 2002-2006

Graduates - All U.S. Medical Schools		Class of 2002	Class of 2003	Class of 2004	Class of 2005	Class of 2006
Women	Race/Ethnicity					
	Black	689	670	642	691	733
	Native American (incl AK)	63	47	43	46	78
	Asian	1,350	1,429	1,458	1,465	1,630
	Native Hawaiian/OPi	22	17	15	21	22
	White	4,237	4,256	4,447	4,539	4,638
	Mexican American	162	161	191	146	175
	Puerto Rican	131	144	152	142	159
	Cuban	0	0	0	0	40
	Other Hispanic	135	143	142	139	168
	Foreign	48	76	76	73	98
	Unknown	88	90	96	153	214
	Total for Women*	6,925	7,033	7,262	7,415	7,746
Men	Race/Ethnicity					
	Black	398	343	391	356	389
	Native American (incl AK)	60	54	56	50	60
	Asian	1,692	1,739	1,713	1,654	1,602
	Native Hawaiian/OPi	33	16	13	25	19
	White	5,808	5,647	5,675	5,495	5,392
	Mexican American	221	188	198	197	185
	Puerto Rican	153	134	154	131	129
	Cuban	0	0	0	1	31
	Other Hispanic	157	180	170	182	176
	Foreign	97	80	77	98	86
	Unknown	136	126	121	161	256
	Total for Men*	8,755	8,507	8,568	8,349	8,179
All Graduates	Race/Ethnicity					
	Black	1,087	1,013	1,033	1,047	1,122
	Native American (incl AK)	123	101	99	96	138
	Asian	3,042	3,168	3,171	3,119	3,232
	Native Hawaiian/OPi	55	33	28	46	41
	White	10,045	9,903	10,122	10,034	10,030
	Mexican American	383	349	389	343	360
	Puerto Rican	284	278	306	273	288
	Cuban	0	0	0	1	71
	Other Hispanic	292	323	312	321	344
	Foreign	145	156	153	171	184
	Unknown	224	216	217	314	470
	Total for Women & Men*	15,680	15,540	15,830	15,764	15,925

Source: AAMC: Data Warehouse: Applicant Matriculant File (DW:AMF) as of 4/18/2007 and SRS_READ_STUDENT_ENROLL_STATUS as of 11/9/06.

* Starting in 2002-03, applicants could indicate races and ethnicities in combination or alone, thus the counts may not be equal to total individual count.

CPSIA information can be obtained
at www.ICGtesting.com
Printed in the USA
BVHW03s2237180218
508433BV00001BA/158/P